Famous Biographies for Young People

FAMOUS AMERICAN POETS

FAMOUS VIOLINISTS FOR YOUNG PEOPLE

FAMOUS PIANISTS FOR YOUNG PEOPLE

FAMOUS COMPOSERS FOR YOUNG PEOPLE

MODERN COMPOSERS FOR YOUNG PEOPLE

FAMOUS MEN OF MEDICINE

FAMOUS AUTHORS FOR YOUNG PEOPLE

FAMOUS EXPLORERS FOR YOUNG PEOPLE

FAMOUS GENERALS AND ADMIRALS FOR YOUNG PEOPLE

FAMOUS KINGS AND QUEENS FOR YOUNG PEOPLE

FAMOUS PIONEERS FOR YOUNG PEOPLE

FAMOUS BRITISH NOVELISTS

FAMOUS BRITISH POETS

FAMOUS MODERN AMERICAN NOVELISTS

FAMOUS INVENTORS FOR YOUNG PEOPLE

FAMOUS AMERICAN NEGROES

FAMOUS OLD MASTERS OF PAINTING

FAMOUS NATURALISTS

FAMOUS AMERICAN STATESMEN

FAMOUS HUMANITARIANS

FAMOUS SCIENTISTS

FAMOUS WOMEN OF AMERICA

FAMOUS WOMEN SINGERS

FAMOUS ENGINEERS

FAMOUS SIGNERS OF THE DECLARATION

FAMOUS NEGRO MUSIC MAKERS

FAMOUS AMERICAN PAINTERS

FAMOUS AMERICAN MEN OF LETTERS

Famous American Men of Letters

by Robert Cantwell

ILLUSTRATED BY GERALD MC CANN

Dodd, Mead & Company

NEW YORK

1956

Contents

JAMES FENIMORE COOPER, *The Sense of the Wilderness* 9

WASHINGTON IRVING, *Humorist and Historian* 25

WILLIAM PRESCOTT, *The Conquest of Mexico* 37

NATHANIEL HAWTHORNE, *Thought and Imagination in Everyday Life* 49

EDGAR ALLAN POE, *Science and Fantasy* 61

RALPH WALDO EMERSON and HENRY DAVID THOREAU, *Concord's Philosopher and Naturalist* 75

HERMAN MELVILLE, *Epic of the Sea* 91

FRANCIS PARKMAN, *Historian of the Wilderness* 103

MARK TWAIN, *The Humor of America* 115

STEPHEN CRANE, *Action and Adventure* 135

O. HENRY, *Millions of Heroes* 149

JACK LONDON, *Melodrama* 161

MODERN AMERICAN WRITERS 173

INDEX 188

*This book is dedicated
with love to my daughter*
Gooden Cantwell

James Fenimore Cooper
1789-1851

James Fenimore Cooper

THE SENSE OF THE WILDERNESS

 1789-1851

JAMES FENIMORE COOPER opened *The Last of the Mohicans* with a scene in the depth of the forest on a hot July afternoon. There were the occasional lazy taps of a woodpecker, the discordant cry of a blue jay. Otherwise, the forest was silent, "that breathing silence which marks the drowsy sultriness of an American landscape in July."

Here, in a setting that every American of the time knew by heart, the novelist pictured a small party threading its way in single file along a dim path under the trees. Among them was a young officer who was conducting two girls to their father at Fort William Henry on Lake George. There was a treacherous Indian guide, Magua, who had led them astray until they were lost. Somewhere in the thickets near by lurked a small band of Indians, no more than ten, bent on scalps and plunder, waiting for darkness to attack.

Near Glens Falls, where the Hudson River drops sixty feet, the wayfarers met a great hunter, called Hawkeye by the Indians, who was modeled on a real American, Daniel Boone. With Hawkeye were two extraordinary characters, Chingachgook and his son, Uncas, the last of the Mohicans.

The story swept on with the speed and power of the

9

river racing through the gorge. Night fell with terrifying rapidity. The shadows thickened in the forest gloom while the sky was still light overhead. In the deceptive light, each waving bush looked like a human form. With merciless haste, Hawkeye and his two Indian friends killed a colt, lest it betray their presence to the Iroquois, and threw its carcass into the river. The horses were tied so they stood in the stream, to mislead the Indians. Then the party took shelter in a cavern below the falls. So real and vivid was Cooper's description that generations of Americans grew up believing that there was a cavern below Glens Falls, but there is none—or, if there ever was one, it has long since disappeared.

In scenes like these, James Fenimore Cooper created something new in literature. Here at home, in the woods that for centuries had been the terror of the settlers in America, he found all the ingredients of romance. One after another, his novels astonished his countrymen by their transformation of the ordinary, tedious or hazardous stuff of common experience into epics of adventure. With tireless inventiveness, Cooper pictured the great woodsman Natty Bumppo —or Hawkeye, as the Indians called him, or Leather-Stockings, as he was sometimes known—scouting, hunting, fighting, escaping, rescuing the lost, saving beleaguered garrisons, talking with the red men in their grave and poetic fashion, or outwitting their best warriors at their own style of warfare.

With tireless descriptive power, Cooper sketched in the settings where Hawkeye (or someone like him) lived and worked: scenes like the farmhouses and rough cabins of Westchester in *The Spy*, Concord and Lexington and Bunker Hill in *Lionel Lincoln*, the wild country around Otsego Lake in central New York in *The Pioneers*. But principally, with effortless immediacy and constant interest, Cooper painted the forest—groves and thickets, woodland meadows and shadowy streams, rocky bluffs and hidden lakes—a wonderland quickened by the alert and vibrant wild life that possessed it, differing in every hill and glade, and yet always alike, an endless haven to which fugitives could flee in times of danger, an immense park and wild playground which could, in an instant, become dark with menace and savagery. This vision of the American wilderness that emerged from Cooper's novels was one of the great imaginative achievements of early American literature. No novelist before him had seen that the woods themselves were a subject for fiction.

⌐James Fenimore Cooper was born on September 15, 1789, in Burlington, New Jersey, but when only a year old was taken into the heart of the wilderness. The first of his ancestors to come to the New World had been James Cooper, who was born in Stratford-on-Avon, the birthplace of Shakespeare. He settled in New Jersey in 1679. His descendants became merchants in Pennsylvania and New Jersey. James Fenimore Cooper's father traveled three hundred miles from his home in Burlington until he came to Lake Otsego, the source of the Susquehanna River, about sixty miles west of Albany.

There Judge Cooper founded a town, Cooperstown, known to all American boys today because the Baseball Hall of Fame is located there. At Cooperstown, Judge Cooper built a great mansion, Otsego Hall. The main hall was fifty feet long, twenty-four feet wide, and had a fifteen-foot high ceiling. By 1805, Judge Cooper had bought so much of the wild land around that he believed himself to be the largest landowner in America.

James Fenimore Cooper was the next to the youngest of a family of thirteen children. The Indians still hunted and traded near by in his early years—there was once fear of an Indian raid—and he accepted as a matter of course the hazards of the wilderness along with the wilderness pleasures that fill his books. After studying four years under an Episcopal clergyman in Albany, Cooper entered Yale at thirteen, left three years later, sailed on a merchantman on an eleven-month voyage, and received his commission as a midshipman in the navy at nineteen. He was one of a party sent to Lake Ontario to build a sixteen-gun brig. There he fell in with the Indian who became the model for the last of the Mohicans. Modern scholars believe that he was Captain Hendrick Aupaumut, who had been one of Washington's secret agents.

Cooper served on the *Wasp* under Captain James Lawrence, the naval hero later remembered for his dying words during the War of 1812: "Don't give up the ship!" In December, 1809, Cooper's father was murdered, and Cooper resigned his commission soon afterward. A member of the legislature, Cooper's father was leaving a political meeting in Albany when he was struck on the head from behind by a political opponent, and died as a result of the blow.

On New Year's Day, 1811, James Fenimore Cooper married Susan Augusta de Lancy, the daughter of a British officer who had served with the British forces during the Revolution. Having inherited $50,000, together with his share of his father's $700,000 estate, Cooper bought land at Scarsdale, near his father-in-law's home north of New York City, and became a gentleman farmer. He lived comfortably, rode horseback over his lands, and in a brilliant blue and gold uniform served as military aide to the governor of New York. There seemed to be nothing serious about him, and no one would have expected him to become a writer.

One night, as he was reading an English novel to his wife,

he threw it aside and said he could write a better one himself. She laughed and challenged him to do so, saying she could not even get him to answer a letter.

As a joke, Cooper wrote *Precaution*. It was a half-burlesque, supposedly the work of an English lady, laid in England, and dealt with the elaborate maneuvers of parents trying to marry their daughter to a young man who is alarmed by their intrigues.

The manuscript was read to family friends, the John Jays, who lived in near-by Bedford. Jay urged Cooper to publish it. Cooper did so, under a pseudonym, and to his surprise the book was a moderate success.

Jay then suggested to Cooper the subject of a serious novel. Now seventy-five years old and a former governor of New York, John Jay had served during the Revolution as the head of a committee of Congress in charge of secret agents and intelligence. One of his best spies had lived in the very region they now inhabited. Many times he had passed through the lines disguised as a peddler. Trusted by the British and hated and feared by most Americans, who did not know his real services, the spy had served with unrewarded heroism, and refused the bag of gold that Congress awarded him after the war. The story made a profound impression on Cooper. He wrote it in *The Spy* during the summer of 1821 and published it anonymously that winter. The book became an immediate success, and was soon translated in most European languages.

In *The Pioneers* (1823), Cooper first introduced the figure of Natty Bumppo, or Leather-Stockings. Only five of the many novels that Cooper wrote belong in the Leather-Stocking series: *The Pioneers, The Last of the Mohicans* (1826), *The Prairie* (1826), *The Pathfinder* (1840) and *The Deer-*

slayer (1841). But in these five novels Cooper fashioned a native type of human being that fixed itself imperishably in American popular culture. In the best of his other books, like *The Pilot* (1824), there were characters akin to Natty Bumppo, just as Harvey Birch in *The Spy* is cut in the same pattern. All were laconic, natural, simple, capable and courageous men, unaffected, inherently democratic and with a great natural dignity. The critic Van Wyck Brooks has pointed out that Leather-Stockings possessed the qualities that the American people later came to admire in Abraham Lincoln. In an odd and almost accidental way, James Fenimore Cooper was creating the American equivalent of misty folk heroes, in the pattern of King Arthur or Roland or the ageless heroes of Homer; and the kind of story he told has persisted, in popular novels and wild West stories and later in radio programs and movies, ever since his time.

So great was Cooper's popular success that 3,500 copies of *The Pioneers* were sold before noon on the day it was published. Within a week five printers were at work bringing out new printings. He moved to New York City on the crest of a wave of triumph. The Secretary of State, Henry Clay, anxious to show the government's appreciation of Cooper's work, offered him the post of Minister to Sweden. Cooper refused it but accepted the unimportant and unpaid post of consul at Lyons, France. There were no duties attached to this job, but as Cooper would be an official of the United States, he would enjoy the privileges of a foreign service officer while still being free to travel around Europe as he pleased.

In 1828, after publishing a sea story, *The Red Rover*, Cooper and his family began their leisurely tour of Europe. Seven years passed before their return to the United States.

They first wandered from one country to another; and Cooper, studying what people said and thought about Americans, wrote *Notions of the Americans* (1828) in which he described popular misconceptions held by Europeans and tried to answer them. Later, while living in Rome and Dresden, he also wrote historical novels with European settings. And he was constantly gathering material for a series of travel books that he published soon after his return to the United States.

Cooper did not understand the changes that had taken place in his absence. Many Americans had been deeply offended by his *Notions of the Americans*. To later generations, much that Cooper said has seemed valid, but the citizens of the young and growing republic were in no mood to brook any criticism. Always combative, Cooper made the conflict worse by publishing *Home As Found*, an unsparing account of how the United States appeared to one who had lived for years in cultivated European circles.

He also purchased Otsego Hall, which had fallen into decay, and restored it. There he lived like the lord of a manor. At this time an extraordinary misunderstanding arose. The villagers had long used a part of the old Cooper estate known as Three Mile Point as a picnic ground. Permission had always been given by Cooper's father, and had continued until it came to be accepted as a right. Cooper's father had left the land to his descendants until 1850, after which it was to become the property of the youngest child bearing his name. James Fenimore Cooper was the executor of his father's estate. He was perfectly willing to let the people use the land for a park, as they had in the past, but he believed it was his responsibility to see that the ownership should not be placed in doubt, so it could be passed on as his father's will provided.

Under certain circumstances, land that was used by the public could be claimed as public property. Cooper therefore posted a notice at Three Mile Point to indicate it was private property, thus complying with the law.

From this trivial incident there rose a storm that nearly destroyed him, and did destroy much of his popularity. In one sense his reputation never recovered, and he is still often described as haughty and aristocratic because of what happened. The townsmen held a meeting to denounce him and his works. They demanded that his books be removed from the public library. The local newspaper published a libelous account of the incident, and Cooper sued the editor.

He won this suit and received damages of $300. But when his next book appeared, other editors denounced him as an aristocrat and a traitor. The most influential literary editor of the time called Cooper "the craziest loon that ever was suffered to roam at large without whip and keeper."

Cooper sued for libel at each of these attacks. For the next five years he was constantly involved in libel suits. He brought them as a matter of principle, believing no private citizen in America should be attacked as he was. He won almost all his cases. The damages awarded, never more than $400, were trivial in terms of the time and expense required. Knowing that Cooper would sue for libel, many irresponsible editors deliberately provoked him and created newspaper discussions to arouse interest in their papers. One editor even kept a running column of libels against Cooper that appeared in other newspapers, printing them all, with Cooper suing each time the column appeared. The cases were delayed, postponed, and dragged on for years, but Cooper never backed down. Finding that he would not stop suing, the editors finally ceased to bait him. His one-man campaign was influential in forcing American newspapers to be more responsible in what they published. However, his personal popularity steadily dwindled, his name was never mentioned in the newspapers he fought, and his books were never reviewed.

Cooper's *History of the Navy of the United States*, published in 1839, also brought a storm of unwarranted abuse upon him. The reason for it is revealing. Cooper's biographer, William Clymer, says rightly that the book is a classic, though unread. Yet in its own time, Cooper's *History of the Navy* was taken by many influential people as a personal affront, and by others as a treasonable disparagement of American heroes.

As the nation grew stronger, American historians wanted to pay full tribute to the military victories won by their country. Influenced by European models and by the histories of antiquity, they pictured the smallest engagements of the Revolution or the War of 1812 as if they were clashes of vast armies and huge fleets. American generals, who were farmers or surveyors in their ordinary life, were depicted in these books as mighty strategists and powerful orators who addressed their troops like the heroes of ancient Rome as they went into battle. James Fenimore Cooper opposed this romanticizing of war in America. In his first serious novel, *The Spy*, he showed war as different in the United States—not the clash of large armies alone, but a curious kind of war that went all through society, a war in which small bands of soldiers were constantly in motion, and with the loyalty of the people going to one side or another. The battles that Cooper described were not like the meeting of Napoleon and Wellington at Waterloo; they were more nearly like Indian battles in the forest, almost hand-to-hand engagements. The naval battles that Cooper analyzed in his *History of the Navy* were not tremendous engagements between fleets of many vessels—nothing like Lord Nelson's decisive victory over the French fleet at Trafalgar—but meetings between small ships, quickly decided. Cooper paid full tribute to the heroism, the daring and skill of American sailors, but he would not delude himself or his readers into thinking that a fight between two small boats on the Great Lakes was the equivalent of the defeat of the Spanish Armada.

In particular, Cooper's account of the Battle of Lake Erie in the War of 1812 aroused his critics to fury. Commodore Perry had won that victory at a low point in the fortunes of the United States, and his famous message—"We have met the enemy and they are ours"—thrilled a generation of Americans. Cooper's matter-of-fact, hard-bitten account that placed the battle in perspective seemed to his readers (especially members of the Perry family and historians who wrote glowing studies of the victory) to be insulting. Their attacks on Cooper's history became so fierce that Cooper was forced to sue. These were not libel cases like those he had won before. They were great court battles. Cooper himself addressed the court for six hours on one occasion, defending his version of the Battle of Lake Erie and challenging the right of his critics to pose as authorities. Cooper vindicated his work, but his standing with the public again suffered.

In his legal battles, Cooper's most vigorous opponent was Captain Alexander Slidell Mackenzie, a once famous and now forgotten naval historian who took the opposite side. Captain Mackenzie was related to the Perry family. In 1842, he became involved in a ghastly mystery. As captain of the *Somers*, commanding a crew of midshipmen on a training cruise, Captain Mackenzie somehow became convinced that the boys were planning a mutiny. Some of those accused were in their early teens. Mackenzie held a hasty trial and hanged two of them. One was the son of the Secretary of War. (Acting with Mackenzie in this tragedy was Guert Gansevoort, a cousin of the novelist Herman Melville.) The scandal of the *Somers* case aroused the whole country. James Fenimore Cooper plunged into battle again. As a former naval officer, Cooper understood what was at stake, and he was determined to show that abuses of authority, while they might be taken for granted under older systems of government, should not be in the United States. Cooper's argument is unanswerable. He demolished Mackenzie's defense of his action. His book on the tragedy of the *Somers* still remains the final word on a dark and mysterious episode of American history.

When Cooper's popularity was at its lowest point, he wrote two more novels of the Leather-Stocking series—*Deerslayer* and *Pathfinder*—and almost recovered his old standing with the public. In the ten years before his death, which occurred on September 14, 1851, he wrote sixteen books, including *The Sea Lions* and *Oak Openings*, which are ranked with his best work.

However, Cooper's long quarrels and his detachment from the contemporary literary scene had made him a little like the last of the Mohicans himself in these years. He lived with his family in seclusion on a farm near Cooperstown. He wrote in the morning and then busied himself clearing more ground, removing stumps, setting out trees, and raising poultry and livestock. He was so kind to the farm animals that they followed him around as he walked over his acres. As he grew tired of the strife that followed the publication of his books and took up so much of his energy, he became more and more engrossed in farming alone. His family life was warmly affectionate. He was deeply religious by nature and in his last year was confirmed in the Episcopal church.

Cooper's influence is almost incalculable. The Leather-Stocking novels made him one of the most popular novelists in history. His works transformed European ideas of life in the New World. The German translations alone are credited with stimulating the immigration of settlers who did so much to develop the Midwest. Sir Walter Scott, the greatest of romantic novelists, at once recognized Cooper as an equal. The famous French author Balzac, the greatest of realistic novelists, praised in the highest terms the originality and grandeur of Cooper's character of Leather-Stockings, "who will live as long as literature lives."

For Cooper had created the first native American hero on a grand scale. In his good-natured, high-spirited, careless and combative fashion, James Fenimore Cooper wrote an epic, with the mysterious and yet familiar woods as the legendary background, and Leather-Stockings as the folk hero. It was an American epic, formless and incomplete, with the trivial and the heroic artlessly intermingled, but a true epic nevertheless. And Leather-Stockings was different from the folk heroes of the Old World. An English critic said there was something Biblical "in the dignity and simplicity of the old backwoodsman . . . with his naïve vanity and strong reverent piety, his valiant wariness, his discriminating cruelty, his fine natural sense of right and wrong, his rough limpid honesty, his kindly humor, his picturesque dialect, and his rare skill in woodcraft . . ."

But as Balzac said, it is the whole magnificent pattern of Cooper's work that arouses admiration—the vision that united the forest, the Indians, the implacable, lifesaving Deerslayer, into a succession of plunging narratives. In detail, from incident to incident, Cooper's novels sometimes grow monotonous and confusing. The same kind of happening occurs again and again. Mark Twain said that whenever a character is alone in the woods in a Cooper novel, surrounded by Indians waiting to scalp him, and in such a desperate fix that he wouldn't make a sound for five dollars, he invariably steps on a twig. Such criticism is justified. It is easy to make fun of Cooper, just as it was easy to make fun of the nobility, the self-sacrifice and the occasional unreality of the Indian hero of *The Last of the Mohicans*. Like his own great creation, James Fenimore Cooper was sometimes too noble, too intelligent, too kindly and courageous to be believable. Yet he was generally right in his long conflicts with his contemporaries. His judgment was sound; and though he was sometimes hot-tempered and tactless, he was also fair, and his integrity was heroic. His simple honesty pervades his books. There is a morning freshness in them, like that of the woods at dawn. They summon up an age of simple conflict, of people too hard pressed to be complicated, of stirring events against the magnificent background of the age-old woods. It is impossible to read Cooper's works and not sense the savor, the thrill and the danger of the wilderness in those early days, and it is scarcely possible to understand early American history without knowing what the immensity of the forest meant to the first Americans.

Washington Irving

 1783-1859

Washington Irving

HUMORIST AND HISTORIAN

 1783-1859

Washington Irving said that when he was a child he was almost obsessed by the lack of stories connected with the life around him, and that whenever he heard of anything strange and unusual happening in New York—a place where a crime was said to have been committed or a house where a ghost had reportedly been seen—he hurried there at once and fixed the scene in his memory.

The youngest of eleven children, he was born in New York City on April 3, 1783, of middle-class Scottish parents. His father, Deacon William Irving, had been a packet officer from the Orkneys before coming to America. During the American Revolution he was so zealous a patriot that he was forced to flee to New Jersey with his family when the British forces approached New York.

Washington Irving's mother, Sarah Sanders Irving, was the granddaughter of an English curate. The atmosphere of the Irving home was always religious and literary. Precocious, undersized and extremely sensitive as a child, the first American writer to receive world recognition had only a fragmentary education in various seminaries in New York. His earliest recollections were of games and play with his brothers and sisters in the garden of their home at 128 William Street. George Washington, for whom he was named, was his early idol, and at the time of Washington's inauguration as first President of the United States, his nurse is reputed to have secured the General's blessing for her charge.

Washington Irving liked to listen to the literary talk of his brothers, William and Peter, who were both members of the Calliopean Society, one of the literary clubs of the time. He spent hours looking through the books of John Newbery, the pioneer printer of books for children, and studying prints of the Thames and London Bridge in *The Gentleman's Magazine*. But the real influence during his formative years was the friendly ferment of the growing city. He mingled with the frocked gentlemen and velvet-clad ladies who paraded around City Hall when Congress was in session, for New York was then the national capital. Or with his dog and gun he tramped along the open country of the Hudson, getting acquainted with "this glorious river." Sometimes he wandered into the Dutch part of the city and listened with awe to the quaint tales told by the descendants of the old Dutch settlers. When Irving was a little older, he frequently climbed secretly at night over his gabled roof to steal away to the little theatre on John Street.

Irving studied law but scarcely practiced it. He was a popular favorite all his life, with his company always sought and his amusing comments always repeated. He dashed off his first writings as a joke and published them anonymously as *The Letters of Jonathan Oldstyle, Gent.* in a newspaper supporting Aaron Burr that was published by Irving's brother Peter. Surrounded by witty young New Yorkers like himself, indulgently regarded by his family, with ample means and a real gift for social life, Irving was under no compulsion to make his way by writing. It was not strange that Irving's contribution to the *Salmagundi Papers* merely reflected his opinions and prejudices (though it also revealed his naturally graceful literary style), or that his first full-length book, *Knickerbocker's History of New York from the Beginning of the World*, was largely an elaborate spoofing of the old Dutch settlers.

It was strange, in fact, that he became a writer at all. Sent abroad by his family for his health, he studied painting. Later, in 1808, a directory of New York listed *Washington Irving, attorney at law, 3 Wall Street*, but his only case was Burr's trial for treason, in which he served in a very minor capacity. When he again went abroad, in 1815, to manage the Liverpool branch of the family hardware business, he became as popular in England as he had been at home, a friend of such famous writers as Sir Walter Scott and Lord Byron.

The carefree happiness of Irving's early years was blighted by the sudden death from tuberculosis of the girl to whom he was engaged. This was a lasting sorrow to him, and though his biographers over-romanticized its effect, there is no question but the direction of his life was changed by her loss. As he said beautifully, "She died in the flower of her youth and mine, but she has lived for me ever since in all womankind." As Irving grew older, gossip linked one name after another with that of "America's most eligible bachelor." Even when he was quite an old man there were repeated rumors that he was to marry one beauty after another. As Irving was then famous, the discussions were not limited to his own circle, but became a favorite topic with the public at large. One of the girls thus assigned to him as an intended wife was Rebecca Gratz, the beautiful Philadelphia girl who served as a model for Rebecca in Scott's *Ivanhoe;* and others included Theodosia Burr, Mary Shelley, a former sweetheart of the poet Robert Burns, and the ex-Empress Maria Louisa.

The failure of his brothers' business in 1817 forced Washington Irving to write for a living. Sir Walter Scott directed him to the wealth of legendary and supernatural material in German literature. Within a year after Irving began the study of German, he completed the first draft of *The Sketch Book*, with the wonderful stories of *Rip Van Winkle* and *The Legend of Sleepy Hollow*.

Irving's *Sketch Book* became the first American literary work to make an impression abroad. His graceful and cadenced style, saved from monotony by his unexpected images and his unerring sense of apt phrases, was the equal of the great English stylists; and there was an odd, original, delightful quality in his intermingling of romantic landscapes and quirky characters that suffused all his writing.

Irving duplicated in England and Europe the social and literary success he had known in New York. He rose from rags to riches in a twinkling, like a fantastic character in one of his own legends. He spent a year enjoying social life in Paris and Dresden. Then he returned to England and worked the overflow of his notes and sketches, the material he had left over when he completed *The Sketch Book*, into *Bracebridge Hall*, which he published in 1822. These sentimental sketches of a countryside that never existed delighted his English followers, and he was soon "hand-in-glove with nobility and mobility." Actually, as important as these works are in American literary history, and as lively as *The Sketch Book* still remains, Irving's achievement in them was not remarkable. He was still drawing on his memories of his youth and retelling the stories that had formed in his mind then. Literary cultivation and knowledge of the world gained in his years abroad gave a polish to his work. His native tales were told with Old World art.

Irving's remarkable achievement was rather in the years that followed. What marked Irving as fundamentally different from the casual wits and humorists of his time was the profound labor that lay back of his books. He might have been expected to settle to another year of social activity, then retire to turn out another work like his last, with constantly thinning inspiration. Instead, he settled in Madrid, in the home of the American consul, and began his magnificent study of Columbus. He revealed a historian's instinctive touch, an uncanny skill in winnowing the Spanish archives that are still baffling to scholars.

The four-volume work, called *The History of the Life and Voyages of Christopher Columbus,* did not appear until 1828. It remained the standard work in its field for a century. Irving was constantly worried for fear subsequent discoveries would invalidate his work. But he did his research with so sure a sense of historical perspective that the most profound of investigations have not discredited his account. Artistically, the book is disappointing. In the words of the historian William Prescott, it is "beautiful, but fatiguing," since the discovery of America takes place early in the narrative, and much that follows is anticlimactic.

A fortunate appointment as secretary of the American legation in London freed Irving of the necessity of earning money by his pen. It was a purely honorary post, given to him so he would have leisure to write.

Washington Irving had shown himself to be a stylist and a historian; he now revealed, in *The Conquest of Granada* (1829), that he was also a subtle writer with a genius for choosing apt and yet unexpected subjects. The mannered form of the book has weakened its appeal, but in its own time it awakened Americans to the strangeness and splendor of Moorish civilization in a way that a straightforward historical narrative could never have done. Two years later, Irving brought out *The Voyages and Discoveries of the Companions of Columbus*, completing his somewhat long-drawn-out cycle of the discovery; and in 1832 he ended his study of the Moors in Spain with *The Alhambra*, sketches revolving around the magnificent palace that had been built by Christian slaves.

He returned to the United States that same year, after an absence of seventeen years. Now forty-nine years old, and one of the world's renowned authors, he felt himself to be like Rip Van Winkle, blinking in wonder at the changes in his native land. He felt he had stepped from darkness into brilliant sunshine of inspiring purity, into a country "where all is life and animation; where I hear on every side the sound of exultation; where everyone speaks of the past with triumph, the present with delight, the future with growing and confident anticipation."

Traveling through the Eastern states in order to catch up with the changing country, he joined a government expedition that proceeded into the West, as far as Oklahoma, a part of the country that was then almost unknown.

Returning to New York by way of New Orleans, Irving wrote *A Tour of the Prairies*, published in 1835. He was determined never again to leave the United States. North of New York, near the Hudson River, in country he had immortalized in *The Sketch Book*, he built his famous home, Sunnyside.

Two more Western books, *Astoria* (1836), dealing with the establishment of a fur-trading settlement at the mouth of the Columbia River, and *The Adventures of Captain Bonne-*

ville, based on the unpublished journals of a famous Western explorer, kept Irving busy until 1838. He then started work on his long-deferred project: the history of the conquest of Mexico. He counted on the book to provide him with bread and butter, for his finances had become troubling. The subject had fascinated him since boyhood. One day he went to New York to look up some material in the Society Library. The librarian told him that William Prescott, a brilliant young historian of Boston who was just beginning to be known, was working on a book about Cortez.

Irving at once gave up the subject to Prescott. He made a greater sacrifice than Prescott ever knew, for Irving had no other subject to which he could turn. Worse still, he found that having set aside his inspiration while actively engaged in writing, he could not recover it when he tried to write of something else. He felt that he never again fully recovered the impetus he had lost. Yet he recognized that Prescott was a better writer for the subject than he himself. "When I made the sacrifice," he wrote, "it was not with a view of compliments or thanks, but from a warm and sudden impulse. I am not sorry for having made it."

In 1842, Irving was appointed Minister to Spain. After four years in Madrid, he wrote his *Life of Oliver Goldsmith*, and in 1849 published another work that showed his genius in choosing the apt subject: *The Lives of Mahomet and His Successors*.

This lively and picturesque book about the founders of Islam took on an added meaning because it was linked to Irving's books on the Moors in Spain and traced back to the founder of Mohammedanism the Arab conquest which had indirectly resulted in Columbus' expedition.

Irving was now an elderly man, serene, universally respected. He began his life of George Washington, intending to make it the culmination of his life work, his masterpiece. But his strength was fading, and he found it more exhausting to establish the facts of Washington's life than it had been for him to appraise confidently the perplexing documents on Columbus. The mellowness that had settled on him and pervaded his writing also was at odds with the life of action found in Washington's career. For five years, he labored on the book, but when it finally appeared, in 1855, it seemed anticlimactic, a thorough, scrupulous job, flawless in its execution, like all Irving's books, still essential reading for all students of Washington's life, but nevertheless lacking in some quality that it should possess. In effect, Irving had written from too tranquil a point of view. What was missing was a sense of all that was at stake in Washington's career—not merely Washington's own victory or defeat, but the defeat or the victory of a new kind of society that might or might not be built in the New World.

Before his death on November 28, 1859, at Sunnyside, Irving declared that he was "the most fortunate old bachelor in the world." His nieces cared for him devotedly and filled his house with youth and gaiety. He remained as good company as ever, and admirers who called to honor him as a great writer found themselves amused by his spontaneous humor and his shrewd common sense. In his lifetime, world opinion on American literature had been completely transformed, and Irving had been to a great extent responsible for the transformation. He was unique in his ability to combine his serious work with his genial humor. When he wrote his great story of Rip Van Winkle, he retained the carefree inconsequence of his jokes in the outlandish events of the tale—old Rip falling asleep for twenty years and awakening in bewilderment at the changes around him—but Irving combined it with a true picture of the countryside, a real understanding of the early New Yorkers and a pointed commentary on the swift changes in American life. The preposterous legend of the headless horseman of Sleepy Hollow became an integral part of the country above New York where it was laid. When Irving wrote the ghost story of Dolf Heylinger spending the night alone in a haunted house on the Hudson, he was principally concerned with writing a ghost story, and he made it a wonderful one, mounting to a climax as the boy hears the heavy tramp of boots on the stairs and sees the bedroom door opening. But Irving also gave a realistic picture of the house itself, the native scenery around it and the habits and speech of the Dutch colonists. He retained his humor when he wrote of serious matters, and his seriousness in his lightest tales, as few writers have been able to do in either the Old World or the New.

William Prescott
1796-1859

William Prescott

THE CONQUEST OF MEXICO

1796-1859

Twenty-eight years after Columbus discovered America, a thirty-four-year-old Spanish soldier opened a new period of American history when he destroyed the Aztec empire of Mexico. This achievement of Hernando Cortez was almost as important as that of Columbus himself. He set out in 1518 from Spain with eleven ships, five hundred soldiers, sixteen horses and ten cannons. He burned his ships after landing in the New World so his men could not lose heart and sail for home. He then pacified, defeated or made allies of the Indians near the coast of Mexico, who were subject to the Aztecs. Then he made his way over ten-thousand-foot mountains to Tenochtitlán, the Aztec capital, a city of a hundred thousand people, richer and more splendid than most of the cities of Europe. There he seized the native emperor, Montezuma, and ruled the powerful empire through him. When the greed and folly of his followers brought on a revolt in his absence, Cortez returned and recaptured Tenochtitlán, though he was forced to destroy the city in the process. The fortunes sent back to Spain from Mexico and Peru, and still more the stories of the strange civilizations of the Aztecs and the Incas, awakened Europe to the knowledge that, even though Columbus had not reached the Indies, there was wealth as great and a world as marvelous in the lands that Cortez had conquered.

When William Hickling Prescott began to write *The History of the Conquest of Mexico* in 1838, very little was definitely known about the subject. The standard English work on the Aztecs was by Lord Kingsborough, who had spent a fortune trying to prove they were descended from the lost tribes of Israel. No copies of Kingsborough's work could be found in the United States. When Prescott eventually secured a copy, sent from England, he confessed he was somewhat disappointed by it.

Nor could Prescott travel to Mexico and study the monuments and ruins and the route of the conquistadors. He was almost blind. Actually, Prescott became a historian as the result of a tragic accident. In the fall of 1813, when he was a seventeen-year-old junior at Harvard, he finished his meal in the Harvard Common and was passing out of the room through the doorway when there was some frolicking among the undergraduates still seated at the tables. As he turned to see what was causing the commotion, a large, hard piece of bread, thrown at random, struck him in the eye. By a rare and all but impossible accident, a vital nerve was struck, and he fell unconscious. His eye was instantly blinded. The effect was like that of a brain concussion. Prescott was prostrated, became nauseated, and his pulse grew so feeble that his life was in danger. After he recovered, his remaining eye became infected, and he was threatened with total blindness.

Prescott was born at Salem, Massachusetts, on May 4, 1796. His grandfather had been the colonel of militia in command at the battle of Bunker Hill. His father was a distinguished lawyer. William Prescott went to schools in Salem and Boston, where his family moved in 1808. He was bright, quick to learn, but was not by nature a student. As a child, he haunted the Boston Athenaeum, a fine private library, but it was not because he was bent on study. There were parts of some old suits of armor in the Athenaeum, and William and his schoolmates dressed themselves in helmets and coats of mail and pretended they were knights fighting battles.

In fact, William Prescott was famous, even as a child, for his high spirits and good nature. He enjoyed horseback riding, dancing and all forms of social life. He had intended to study law, but his weak vision made it impossible. He returned to college when he recovered from the accident, and by resolute study was graduated with honors in 1814. He memorized whole pages of his mathematics textbook, without understanding them in the slightest, in order to catch up with his class.

Soon after he was graduated, his right eye became more inflamed. His joints were swollen with rheumatism, and for fifteen weeks he could not walk. When he sailed for the Azores, on September 26, 1815, there was a very real likelihood that he would never return.

William's grandfather, his mother's father, was the United States consul at Ponto Delgada. He had married a Portuguese woman, and built a house he called Yankee Hall. William had barely arrived at his grandfather's home when his sight suddenly became much worse. From November 1 until February 1, 1816, he remained in a room that was totally dark. Fearing that his body would become stiff if he remained inactive, he paced from one corner to the opposite one, until he had walked a hundred miles in his room. He sang in order to keep up his spirits.

When his sight was stronger, he went to England to consult doctors there. They gave him no hope. William was taken around to the famous scenes of England by the American Minister, John Quincy Adams, who was soon to become President.

Back in America, the next few years of William's life were spent trying to adjust himself to a semi-invalid existence. He decided that he must somehow work regularly, to keep his spirits up, but he knew of no kind of work to do. He decided he must keep regular hours, although, as his friend and biographer George Ticknor said, "His nature—buoyant, frolicsome and simplehearted—and his temperament—strong, active and wilful—long contended against his wise determination."

Since boyhood, Prescott had always hated to get up early in the morning, but he now resolved to arise early each day. After he was called, he counted to twenty, very slowly and reluctantly, and if he were not out of bed by the time he reached twenty, he paid a dollar to the servant who called him. If he fell asleep again, the servant was instructed to enter the room, after a few minutes, and carry away all the bedclothes, and William had to pay him more money.

After dressing, he rode horseback. Even on the coldest of New England mornings he rode from the Prescott home on Bedford Street three or four miles beyond the city of Jamaica Plains, where he watched the sunrise.

On May 4, 1820, he married Susan Amory, the daughter of a Boston merchant. Her mother's father had commanded a British ship which fired shells at Prescott's grandfather commanding the Americans on Bunker Hill. The marriage was a very happy one. Prescott and his bride lived for many years with his parents, as his eyesight, while growing stronger, was still very weak. They subsequently built their own home on Beacon Street. Four children were born to them—two girls and two boys. Prescott called one son The Colonel and the other The Judge.

For several years Prescott wrote occasional critical articles, some of which were published and some of which were returned by the editors. His sister, who read to him in preparation for such work, was furious when the articles were returned, but Prescott was modest about his writing and never expected anything he wrote to succeed. He vaguely planned a book on Roman history, showing how the republic became a monarchy, then planned another on Italian literature. His close friend, George Ticknor, was a great Spanish scholar, and interested Prescott in Spain. On January 19, 1826, after much doubt, and with many misgivings, Prescott decided to write a history of the reign of Ferdinand and Isabella.

The story of the Spanish monarchs in whose time Spain had been united, the Moors expelled and the New World discovered, had never been written. Prescott's eyes were so sensitive that he could not read at all. Just as he reached his decision, another attack was so bad that he had to remain four months in complete darkness. He finally resumed work in a room where different thicknesses of blue muslin curtains could be drawn over the windows, according to the degree of sunlight outside. A green screen that could be moved provided additional protection, and he wore a green eyeshade. The coal fire that glowed in the fireplace was not permitted to burst into flame. Prescott's secretary sat behind him and read aloud, the light on his pages shadowed. They worked in this way from ten until two each day and from six until eight each evening.

For the first two years, Prescott studied European history in general: governments, constitutions, commerce, laws, religions. There followed 267 days of more concentrated preparatory study. For a single chapter—the history of the Arabs in Spain—he put in seven and a half months of study. At last, on October 6, 1829, he was ready to begin the first chapter.

In four and a half months the first draft of the first chapter was completed. It was rewritten three times. Prescott planned to finish about two hundred pages a year. After four years, he began printing four copies of the book, in very large type, so that he could read it, with only a few lines on each page. The pages were printed on only one side, with very wide margins on which he wrote corrections.

He used a machine with wires to guide his hand across the page. His secretary then copied his notes and read them to him. For the Arab chapter alone, there were 244 large pages of notes, and these were all indexed. Prescott's memory became so strong he could carry as many as three complete chapters, or seventy-two pages, in his head. He learned to compose in his mind, walking or riding horseback, then to dictate from memory to his secretary.

While he was working on his chapter about the Arabs, his oldest daughter suddenly died, and his grief made it all but impossible for him to continue. Periods of his own illness delayed him. He had a constant struggle to force himself to go on with the work. He made elaborate bets with himself or with his secretary. Sometimes he wagered that he could work every day for a certain period. Another time he made a bet with himself that he could give up an amusement that interfered with work. Once he wagered with his secretary that he could write 250 pages in a year. He always hated to work. He would never tell his secretary what the bets were. Instead, Prescott would write them out on a piece of paper so the secretary could not see what was written on it, and both would sign their names. Prescott on one occasion posted bonds that he would pay $1,000 if he lost. Sometimes he would come in gloomily and pay the secretary $20 (once even $100) because he said the secretary had won, and on one occasion he collected $10 which he said he had won from the secretary.

At last, after seven and a half years, the book was finished. Another year was spent in correcting and revising. On the day the book was published, one of Prescott's friends, who seldom read anything, got up before dawn so he could buy the first copy offered for sale. Many others, who rarely bought books, purchased *Ferdinand and Isabella* because Prescott had written it. They all liked it because they were all fond of Prescott.

What they did not know was that he had produced one of the world's great masterpieces of historical writing—"the book had been born a classic." Soon there came a chorus of praise from scholars in England, France and Spain. Prescott's freshness and vitality, his superb characterizations, the thoroughness of his study and his fine sense of proportion had brilliantly illuminated a period that was all but unknown. There were only a dozen scholars in the world capable of appreciating the tremendous research that had gone into the work. But everyone could appreciate its narrative and color. The publishers planned to sell five hundred copies in five years. These were sold at once. Some 2,800 were sold in the first year and 17,000 within a few years.

The success of *Ferdinand and Isabella* spurred Prescott to further researches and he decided to do a book on Cortez. When Washington Irving heard that Prescott was working on the story of the conqueror of Mexico, he at once gave up his own lifelong plan of doing a book on the subject. His letter to Prescott in which he pretended that the difficulties of research had deterred him almost frightened Prescott into giving up the subject himself, for the problems were enormous. There were few reliable documents. The conquistadors had quarreled so violently that the archives were confused with their conflicting denunciations of each other. The remaining ruins of Aztec civilization were only eerie and perplexing. Only a single authoritative French work, *Antiquitiés Mexicaines*, existed. The explorer Alexander von Humboldt had written an honest account of the surviving fragments of the ancient civilization, and gave Prescott valuable assistance. A great Spanish scholar, Pascual de Gayangos, also gathered material for him.

It was plain that there had been a complex society of mixed savagery and civilization in Mexico before Cortez. There had been nations—not roving Indian tribes—nations with capital cities, armies, courts of justice. There had been great architects who built towering buildings of white stone rising at the edge of lakes, and engineers of skill, who built aqueducts that provided the cities with fresh water. The city of Tenochtitlán itself, built where Mexico City now stands, was an architectural and engineering marvel, built in a lake for protection, with three causeways, thirty feet wide and as long as five miles, connecting it with the mainland.

Within this city there had been factories, producing multicolored cloth from bird feathers by mass-production methods, and huge colonnaded market places with paved stone floors. The homes of whitewashed stone possessed courts, beautiful gardens and elaborately carved woodwork. The palaces contained hundreds of rooms. Montezuma's palace was so large that one of Cortez' companions wandered four times around it, walking until he was tired, without having seen it all. In the gardens there were groves of cypresses, beds of rare plants and zoos containing many kinds of wild animals. The armies were organized into divisions, each containing eight thousand men. Swift runners carried news and messages to all parts of the empire. With an emerging—or decaying—civilization, there was also incredible savagery. In one celebration to the gods, a few years before Columbus' discovery of America, there had been twenty thousand human sacrifices in a single temple.

How had it come about that Cortez and his few men had conquered an empire? Day after day, for years, Prescott worked on the great enigma. Gradually, the picture of what had happened became plain in his mind. He began to see Cortez more and more clearly; and if he could not quite feel confident of seeing ancient Mexico, he understood the Aztecs with whom the Spaniards had been in contact. In five years, Prescott completed his book. *The History of the Conquest of Mexico* was immediately recognized as a classic study, in which the desperate courage of Cortez' small band and the mixed savagery and splendor of the Aztec empire provided a story of unfailing interest.

Prescott was now almost totally blind. The hour of work he was permitted each day had to be divided into periods of a few minutes at a time. Maps were still a terrible problem, but he had mastered his method of work, and at once began *The History of the Conquest of Peru*. *The Conquest of Mexico* was published on December 6, 1843. The companion volume on Peru appeared late in March, 1847. The war with Mexico (1846–1848) increased popular interest in the subject of Prescott's books, so much so that by 1860 the Peru volume alone had sold 16,965 volumes, though it was not nearly so popular as *The Conquest of Mexico*. All Prescott's books were popular, and though he had inherited wealth, with an income of $12,000 a year, his literary labors earned much more, paying him more than $3,000 a month in some periods.

Prescott was asked to write a history of the Mexican War, but decided not to do so. Instead, he published a volume of essays and began his last major work, *The History of Philip the Second*, which was finally published in November, 1857. In 1850, Prescott sailed for England, in what soon developed into the most brilliant visit ever made to that country by an American who was not in an official position. He attended the Court Ball given by Queen Victoria and admitted that he was a little impressed by the "power of diamonds" on display. He then made what amounted to a triumphal procession from one great country house or castle to another, for both the Queen and Prince Albert had indicated to him that they were deeply interested in his work, and Englishmen followed their example.

Prescott died on January 27, 1859. More than any other American historian, and perhaps more than any historian, Prescott possessed the gift of awakening interest in his subjects. Most of the great historians, men like Macaulay and Gibbon, with whom Prescott can be ranked, tended to exhaust the subjects of which they wrote, to answer all the questions, and to give final answers with authority. It was Prescott's gift to stimulate the reader's interest, to make him want to learn more; and his works have inspired study along the paths he blazed and a sympathetic understanding of the lands of which he wrote.

Nathaniel Hawthorne
 1804-1864

Nathaniel Hawthorne

THOUGHT AND IMAGINATION IN EVERYDAY LIFE

1804-1864

NATHANIEL HAWTHORNE was unique among American novelists in that he seemed to know exactly what he wanted to do from the time he began to write. After he was graduated from Bowdoin College in Maine in 1825, he settled in his native town of Salem, Massachusetts, and for twelve years lived in seclusion while he wrote many of the stories that later made him famous. He was not hidden away or anything of the sort; he knew many people and enjoyed himself a good deal. But everything that he published appeared under pseudonyms, and no one knew how great a writer was living quietly in the ancient seaport.

Hawthorne was born in Salem on July 4, 1804. His father was a sea captain who commanded the *Mary Eliza*, the *Neptune*, the *Nabby*, and sailed to Java and the Far East. His mother was Betsy Manning Hawthorne, whose family owned the stagecoach line that ran between Boston and Salem.

When Nathaniel was four years old, his father died of yellow fever while on a voyage to South America. Thereafter Mrs. Hawthorne and Nathaniel and his two sisters made their home with the Manning family. Nathaniel's grandfather Manning owned an enormous tract of land, almost thirty-seven thousand acres, around Lake Sebago in southern Maine. The land was then wilderness, but Mr. Manning was selling portions to settlers, and a small village called Raymond was growing at one end of Lake Sebago. During his childhood, Nathaniel divided his time between the busy port of Salem and the wilderness settlement of Raymond. In Maine he ran as wild as an Indian, swam in Crooked River, fished for trout in Dingley Brook, hunted partridges and squirrels, and once even stalked a bear in the woods.

In Salem he was forced to attend dancing classes, go to school, and mind his clothes and manners. The Hawthorne family was one of the oldest in the city. Several branches were wealthy and were conscious of their social position. An ancient tragedy cast a pall over Salem for any imaginative member of the Hawthorne family. In 1692, during the witchcraft hysteria in New England, nineteen people were put to death in Salem for witchcraft, which meant being in league with the devil. One of Nathaniel's ancestors was a Judge Hawthorne, who was known as the witchcraft judge. As a matter of history, Judge Hawthorne had not had much to do with it. He was a soldier, not a judge, and had merely served as an examining magistrate who passed the cases on to a special tribunal set up to try them. Nevertheless, the horror of the proceedings was attached to his name, all the more since one of the dying women uttered a curse on him and all his descendants.

If Hawthorne could have had his own way, he would have remained in the wilderness all his life, moving on as one part after another became settled. He rarely went to school until he was almost fifteen. Then he was sent to study under the Reverend Caleb Bradley, at Stroudwater, Maine, near Portland, a town he immortalized in a little story years later, *The Vision of the Fountain*. He was prepared for Bowdoin

College by Dr. Benjamin Lynde Oliver, of Salem, an inventor, lens grinder, former professor and retired physician and the greatest chess player in the United States. Between study periods, young Hawthorne worked in the stagecoach office for a salary of a dollar a week.

His college career was uneventful, except that he was once nearly expelled for gambling. But college was important because so many of his friends and classmates there became famous and influential. The poet Henry Wadsworth Longfellow was in his class. His college friend Franklin Pierce became President of the United States. Pitt Fessenden, with whom he gambled, became Lincoln's Secretary of the Treasury. There were congressmen, senators, governors, merchants, judges and even prosperous writers among Hawthorne's college friends—the three Abbott brothers, John, Jacob and Gorham, were all well-known authors, Gorham having written the famous Rollo books. Another college friend became indirectly famous for literary reasons. He was Calvin Stowe, the husband of the woman who wrote *Uncle Tom's Cabin.*

During the twelve years he remained unknown, Hawthorne did not lose heart. He wanted to write stories that would be like European folk tales. The New World lacked the storied associations of the Old. The town of Hamlin was famous for the legend of the Pied Piper. Children knew of Sherwood Forest because they knew of Robin Hood. Hawthorne wanted to write of the familiar places of home, but he wanted his stories to have the simplicity and mystery of folk tales invented ages ago by storytellers now unknown. He said those stories did not seem to have been made but to have grown, to be works of nature rather than works of art—"and certainly," he said, "as long as man exists, they can never perish."

He wanted "to diffuse thought and imagination through the opaque substance of today"—thought to bring out the true and indestructible values that were hidden in everyday life, and imagination to spiritualize the human burden, to contribute something of enjoyment, of grace, of fancifulness, to everyday existence that was so often wearisome and dull. Art as he saw it was not something to exist only on museum walls or in concerts, but should be woven into the very fabric of ordinary living. His aim was a noble one, and it is not surprising that he felt he failed. His first book, *Seven Tales of My Native Land*, written the summer after he was graduated from college, he destroyed. Only one story survived. The next, *Fanshawe*, a novel of college life, he printed at his own expense ($100), then collected all the copies he could find and burned them because the book did not come up to the high standard he had set for himself. Under his various pseudonyms—Reverend Ashley Royce was one—he brought out his finely wrought little tales, constantly working them over, and destroying many more than he published.

Twelve years passed. Hawthorne wrote all day and in the evening walked through the town or down to the beach or climbed Gallow's Hill, where the people accused of witchcraft had been put to death. He read a whole library of the best of English and American literature. He made a few trips around New England, sometimes with an uncle who was buying horses for the stagecoach line.

Sometimes he visited with Horatio Bridge, his closest friend from college days. Occasionally he saw Franklin Pierce, already a famous politician. A few editors knew him as a mysterious contributor of interesting stories who insisted that his identity be kept secret. Hawthorne had some official position of a law-enforcement nature, for he mentions in his note-book (August 18, 1838) that he was called upon to question a woman accused of stealing. When a government powder magazine was blown up in Pittsfield, Massachusetts, Hawthorne visited the area. He traveled under an assumed name, and did not tell anyone where he was going. For several weeks he remained in the neighborhood, walking idly through the country and listening to the talk of the people. He wrote in his notebook that when he joined a group of men talking on the porch of the Whig Tavern in North Adams, one of them looked at him steadily and said, "I do not know your name. But there is something of the Hawkeye about you too."

In these twelve years, Hawthorne began to be haunted by a recurring dream. It seemed to him that he was still in college. All his friends had gone beyond him. He met them while he was still a student, and they were busy men of the world. He felt a sense of humiliation so painful that it remained after he awakened.

He made an effort to get away from his Salem life and became the editor of a magazine in Boston, *The American Magazine of Useful and Entertaining Knowledge*. Aided by his sister Elizabeth, he wrote almost the entire magazine. The publication had virtually failed before he became editor, but he did not know it and worked on desperately, although his salary was not paid. Then the company went bankrupt, and he could not collect the large amount that was due him.

Around 1837, his confidence suddenly gave way. He became so depressed that Horatio Bridge feared he would commit suicide. Without Hawthorne's knowledge, Bridge promised to pay a Boston publisher for any losses he incurred in publishing a book of Hawthorne's stories, to be brought out under his own name, and in this way *Twice-Told Tales* came into being on March 17, 1837.

Hawthorne was never again out of the public eye. A Salem artist, Sophia Peabody, illustrated one of the stories in the book. Hawthorne fell in love with her. Their marriage was a happy one, a son and two daughters being born to them. In the years that followed, Hawthorne had his share of troubles, too, but on the whole he was successful and reasonably prosperous: compared with most American writers, he was fortunate. He worked in the Boston Custom House before his marriage; joined Brook Farm, an experimental co-operative colony; settled in Concord, Massachusetts, where he wrote *Mosses from an Old Manse;* and between 1846 and 1849 held an important post in the Salem Custom House. When a change of administrations forced him out of office, he wrote *The Scarlet Letter*, which became a sensational success. In the three years between 1850 and 1853, while he was living in western Massachusetts, Hawthorne wrote *The House of the Seven Gables*, which many critics believe to be his best book, a story of Salem, revolving around an old house owned by one of his relatives; *The Snow Image*, another collection of his stories; *The Blithedale Romance*, a novel dealing with Brook Farm; *The Wonder Book* and *Tanglewood Tales*, which were retellings in modern terms of the old Greek myths.

When Franklin Pierce became a last-minute candidate for the Presidency in 1852, Hawthorne wrote a campaign biography for his old friend. After Pierce was elected, Hawthorne was appointed consul at Liverpool. The family remained in England until 1855. A trip to Italy gave Hawthorne the subject of his last novel, *The Marble Faun*. The years in England provided the material for *Our Old Home*, which was written during the Civil War, after the Hawthornes had again settled in Concord. Hawthorne's health failed mysteriously during the war; he was unable to finish three very promising novels that he had started; and he died on May 19, 1864, at the age of sixty. The poet Carl Sandburg has written that Hawthorne was one of the many sensitive Americans who were so deeply affected by the tragedy of the Civil War that they literally died of it.

The abiding interest in Hawthorne is in his work. How nearly did he come to achieving the high purpose with which he set out? In his best tales he certainly succeeded in throwing a luminous half-light over the native scene and investing events with a legendary quality. The famous story *The Great Stone Face* is the best-known example of his work, but, as interesting and suggestive as it is, it is inferior in artistry to others. *The Gray Champion*, although it is only a fragment, is actually a kind of synthetic legend. Hawthorne's tales of witchcraft, such as *Alice Doane's Appeal*, *The Hollow of the Three Hills* and *Young Goodman Brown*, effectively transmute the raw material of superstition into moral tales of universal significance. And in his masterpiece, *The Scarlet Letter*, an intense and tragic story of infidelity, he combined an unforgettably realistic picture of the harshness of the Puritans with poetic fancifulness and wonder.

Hawthorne was a very great artist. He was rare in that his artistry was in everything he wrote—in his letters and his notebooks, in his books for children, in his casual journalism, as well as in his most finished works of fiction. He was the first conscious artist among American writers, polishing and repolishing his work. His books seem to shimmer between reality and romance. His characters are a unique compound, partly poetic symbols, partly living and breathing human beings. His scenes are ordinary New England hills and village squares, but bathed in a vague half-light, with a quality that impressed his early critics as being a kind of spirit world, like the reflection of the real world seen on the surface of a lake. At his own distinctive kind of writing, no one has bettered him.

Yet most critics have felt, and Hawthorne himself believed, that there was something incomplete about his writing. He gained the effect he sought at the expense of an impact on the life of his time. In *The Blithedale Romance* he took the story out of the commonplace and the literal and really elevated it into a timeless tragedy—the tragedy of an idealistic reforming spirit twisted by human imperfections. But the more Hawthorne added the legendary quality that is the trade-mark of his books, the less the story meant to the everyday life of his time. Brook Farm itself, as the inspiration of the story, was more significant, more interesting, than the novel it inspired. And so it is with much of Hawthorne's work. No one passing the site of Brook Farm thought of it as the setting of *The Blithedale Romance*. The visitors to the Berkshires never thought of them as the scene of Hawthorne's timeless story of *Ethan Brand*. Even Irving, far less serious in his artistry than Hawthorne, came close to doing what Hawthorne tried to do in linking the tale of the headless horseman with the real place of Sleepy Hollow. Neither Hawthorne nor Irving nor any other American fused place and legend as did the unknown storytellers of the Old World who forever identified the Pied Piper with the town of Hamlin or Dick Whittington and his cat with London town.

But if he had not fully achieved his major purpose, he nevertheless awakened Americans to the loveliness of facets of American life they had never suspected. When Oliver Wendell Holmes read Hawthorne's stories, he exclaimed, "A light falls upon the place, not of land or sea! . . . Oh, the purple light, the soft haze, that now rests on our glaring New England! He has *done* it, and it will never be harsh country again."

Edgar Allan Poe

 1809-1849

Edgar Allan Poe

SCIENCE AND FANTASY

 1809-1849

On June 21 and 28, 1843, there appeared in a weekly magazine called *The Dollar Newspaper* a brilliant and unusual story, *The Gold-Bug*, by Edgar Allan Poe. The illustration showed three figures, partially revealed by lantern light, staring in astonishment into a pit they had dug beneath an enormous tree. And the expressions on their features were justified, for the story related how, at that precise moment, they had found a pirate chest containing $1,500,000 in gold and jewels.

A claim might have been made that *The Gold-Bug*, all things considered, was the most interesting and ingenious short story in American literature up to that time. The chance discovery of an old parchment, with a mysterious cipher written upon it, leads an impoverished young Southerner named Le Grand to put his mind to work, first interpreting the cipher, and then following the complicated directions that are given for finding the treasure. All the interest is purely intellectual. In Poe's story of pirate gold there was no question of pirate battles or escape from shipwreck preceding the finding of the gold. All the interest centered in *how* the secret was discovered, *how* the puzzle was solved, *how* the incredibly baffling directions that led to the chest were fol-

61

lowed. The cipher that Poe worked into his story was a brilliant one. To have compressed it into *The Gold-Bug*, then to have shown the working out of the solution in detail, to have combined it with a vivid narrative of digging in the darkness for the treasure, and to have done so in a few thousand words, made *The Gold-Bug* a terrific demonstration of purely intellectual excitement, a mental feat.

Edgar Allan Poe had no desire, like Hawthorne, to create a legendary hero. He was a legend himself. He was born in Boston on January 19, 1809, the son of a young English-born actress. His father was David Poe, of Baltimore, an actor who was the son of a Revolutionary war hero. Edgar Allan Poe had an older brother, William Henry Leonard Poe, and a younger sister, Rosalie. Their mother was a well-known actress in the early days of the American theatre. She appeared in theatres up and down the Atlantic coast, playing 201 different roles in all and gradually appearing more and more in Shakespearean tragedies.

She died in 1811, at the age of twenty-three. David Poe, the father, is believed to have died the year before. William Henry, the older son, was taken into the home of his grandfather, General David Poe, of Baltimore. Rosalie was adopted by family friends. Edgar Allan Poe was taken into the home of a prosperous tobacco merchant of Richmond, Virginia, named John Allan.

Poe was never adopted by John Allan, though everyone believed that he was to be his heir. Mr. Allan and his pretty, young wife were childless. She was a Richmond girl of excellent family. She loved the orphan she had taken into her home but was not in good health and could not give him the care he should have had. Mr. Allan was born in Scotland and came to Richmond in 1795 to work for his uncle, who was one of the wealthiest merchants in the city.

Poe wrote later that Mr. Allan tried to be kind to him, but that he was naturally a rough character. This seems to have been true. Mr. Allan was a vigorous, hard-hitting, independent man, often traveling to the Azores on business or hurrying north to free one of his ships that had been caught trying to run the embargo. Mr. Allan considered himself an upright and respectable citizen and was extremely severe with Edgar. But there were scandals and mysteries in his life, and his immoralities became most flagrant at the very time he was most strict with Edgar.

As soon as the War of 1812 ended, Mr. Allan took his wife and Edgar to England. There they remained for six years. Edgar Allan Poe was placed in a school in Stoke Newington, a suburb northeast of London, in a shadowy old building behind high brick walls.

Through the impressionable years of his childhood, Edgar lived in the unique atmosphere of this small, secluded English school, in an environment he described as "dream-like and spirit-soothing." Later, American travelers who came upon the school building were startled because it looked so much like the setting of one of Poe's eerie tales. He himself seems to have remembered it as pleasant. The educational standard was high. When Poe returned to Richmond, he was far ahead of boys of his own age in his studies.

Business reverses forced Mr. Allan to return to Richmond in 1822. Edgar Allan Poe was at that time a vigorous, active youth who swam in Shockoe Creek, fished and hunted, and had many friends among the Richmond boys. He was a good athlete, especially at swimming, boxing and running. He was a lieutenant of the Richmond Junior Riflemen and formed part of Lafayette's guard of honor when the French hero visited Richmond in 1824. Lafayette had been a close personal friend of his Grandfather Poe during the Revolution. The earliest letter of Edgar Allan Poe's that has been preserved is a request to the governor of Virginia that the Junior Riflemen be allowed to keep their arms after Lafayette left.

In 1825, shortly before Edgar entered the University of Virginia, Mr. Allan inherited a fortune of $700,000 on the death of the uncle for whom he had worked when he first came to Richmond. He moved to a fashionable neighborhood, to a large house which he purchased from a Spanish merchant. He was angry, however, with Edgar and was guilty of an act of almost incredible cruelty. Edgar was greatly influenced by his older brother William Henry, though they rarely saw each other. William had become a midshipman in the navy, and was at the point of sailing to South America on the *Macedonian*. Mr. Allan wrote to William Henry in Baltimore a letter which was calculated to create bad feeling between him and Edgar and also cast reflection on the boys' mother. The most scrupulous modern biographers have winnowed the records of marriages, births and deaths, and they have found that there is no foundation for the charge that Poe's mother ran away with David Poe within a month of her first husband's death. The original record has also been discovered which proves they were legally married.

Edgar and Mr. Allan had been on bad terms for a long time. They now became enemies. When Edgar entered the University of Virginia in 1826, Mr. Allan would not give him enough money to pay his fees. He was soon heavily in debt and began to gamble. Presently he owed a huge sum, believed to amount to $2,500, in gambling debts. Mr. Allan refused to pay them and removed him from college in disgrace.

After violent quarrels with John Allan, Edgar slipped out of Richmond in disguise, under the name of Henri Le Rennet. He somehow made his way to Boston. There he became friendly with a young printer who published (anonymously) his first book, *Tamerlane and Other Poems*.

Immediately thereafter, Poe enlisted in the army under the name of Edgar A. Perry. He was assigned to Battery H of the First Artillery, and stationed at Fort Independence in Boston Harbor. He was an exemplary soldier. When his company was transferred to Fort Moultrie in Charleston Harbor, South Carolina, Poe was company clerk. His duties were light and he spent much of his time exploring the surrounding country. It was the scene of the story he later wrote, *The Gold-Bug*.

In 1829, Poe was promoted to regimental sergeant major. For three years he had successfully concealed his whereabouts from the people he had known in Richmond. There were stories that he was in Paris, then in Russia, then that he had enlisted in the Turkish army. Poe's early biographers believed these tales of foreign travel and adventure. Later, when they were shown to be false, the impression grew that all Poe's accounts of his early life were fabrications. In recent years, however, it has been discovered that Poe's brother actually had some of the adventures attributed to Edgar Allan Poe, and may have been in Saint Petersburg.

After three years, Poe wrote to Mr. Allan and disclosed where he was. He started for Richmond on a furlough, but before he arrived, Mrs. Allan died. The following year, Mr. Allan married again, and his young wife, unlike the first Mrs. Allan, disliked and distrusted Edgar. There was no possibility of his making his home with the Allans. There followed a difficult period while Poe secured his discharge from the army and won an appointment to West Point.

Mr. Allan did not help him, beyond going through the forms of assistance. But Edgar had acquired friends of his own. He was becoming known to men of letters in Baltimore, where he lived with his widowed aunt, Mrs. Maria Clemm. His superior officers in the army wrote glowing reports on his ability when he applied for his West Point appointment. Old army men remembered the heroic record of his Grandfather Poe. Edgar personally called on the Secretary of War. Early biographers said that General Winfield Scott and Chief Justice John Marshall used their influence to get Poe accepted for West Point, though no proof has been found.

Poe was a good cadet at West Point. His educational background and his long experience in the army made the training easy for him. He was older than most of the cadets. Everything indicated that Poe was at the beginning of a successful career. His brother, William Henry, was back in Baltimore, where he was becoming known as a writer. Suddenly, for no reason that has ever been revealed, Poe forced the authorities to expel him. He merely broke unimportant rules for a week. As he offered no defense when he was court-martialed, discharge was compulsory. As incredible as it seems, the cadets raised a sum of money to help him publish another book of poems. Still stranger is the fact that he remained on good terms with the superintendent of the Academy. The sentence of his court-martial was delivered on January 5, 1831.

By some strange twist of fate, Poe's life had not been disorderly up to this time, but on the record it seemed so. He had been a good student at college and had been removed in disgrace; he had been a good soldier (under a different name); and he had been a good cadet but had been court-martialed and dismissed. And now a still darker episode indicated to some that Mr. Allan's low opinion of him was warranted. He was arrested for debt in Baltimore. Actually, it was not his debt, but a debt of his brother's which he had assumed. His brother was dying of tuberculosis. William Henry Poe's strength had been weakened by drinking—another charge that was soon to be laid at Edgar Allan Poe's door. Rosalie, who was also brilliant as a child, is said to have remained childlike when she grew to womanhood, and is sometimes described as insane before her death in 1874.

Edgar, then, had little of the wild desperation later characteristic of him. He was known as Buddy and was generally well liked, though there was a touchiness about him that kept him from being popular. He was befriended by a group of literary men in Baltimore, several of them men of acute perceptions, and one, at least, John Kennedy, the author of *Swallow Barn* and *Horse-Shoe Robinson*, a novelist of ability. In 1833, Poe won first prize of $100 in a contest run by a weekly newspaper, the *Baltimore Sunday Visitor*, with his story *Ms Found in a Bottle*. Poe had submitted several stories, including the famous *A Descent into the Maelstrom*. The judges of the contest were so impressed that they published an official statement asking that all Poe's stories be brought out in a book, and adding, "These tales are eminently distinguished by a wild, vigorous, and poetical imagination, a rich style, a fertile invention, and varied and curious learning."

Poe became editor of *The Southern Literary Messenger* at a salary of $1,000 a year. He was a brilliant editor and increased the circulation of the magazine from 500 to 3,500 copies before he left it in 1837. He contributed eighty-three reviews, six poems, four essays and three stories to the *Messenger*, and had become famous as the only arresting critic of contemporary literature in the United States.

In 1838, Edgar Allan Poe married his cousin, Virginia Clemm. After living briefly in New York, Poe, his wife and Mrs. Clemm settled in Philadelphia, where he edited *Graham's Magazine* for a year and a half. Under his editorship, the circulation of *Graham's* increased from six thousand to forty thousand subscribers, one of the most spectacular advances in the history of publishing. By this time, Poe was an amazingly successful editor, frank and independent, with an intuitive, curious mind, awake and alert in all directions, with ceaseless interests combined with his fertile inventiveness. He had a gift for making his own direct, commonsensical criticisms, though they were often no more than statements of obvious truths, seem like the extraordinary discoveries of genius. For *Graham's* and other magazines he wrote some of his best stories: *The Murders in the Rue Morgue, The Fall of the House of Usher, The Pit and the Pendulum, The Tell-Tale Heart, The Black Cat, The Mystery of Marie Roget.* Poe also solved cryptograms in the magazine, offering to break any cipher that the readers would send him. Like Sherlock Holmes, he figured out the solution of crimes, deducing who the murderer must be from the facts in the newspapers. From the first chapters of Charles Dickens' novel *Barnaby Rudge,* Poe deduced how the novel was going to turn out. He was so right that Dickens said he must be in league with the devil.

Poe left the magazine, probably as a result of a quarrel with the owners over money, for despite his success he earned only $800 a year. Tragic years in New York followed, where he edited the *Mirror* and *The Broadway Journal* and busied himself trying to raise money to start a magazine of his own. But his health had been breaking down for many years, stories of his dissipations drove away possible supporters, and his savage temper became legendary. He was always in debt, borrowing from well-wishers, plunging into debauchery, or turning to drugs, to try to forget his troubles or to relieve himself of the strain of his intense periods of work. His wife died in January, 1847, and Poe's life became still more disorderly and violent. He died under mysterious circumstances in Baltimore on October 7, 1849.

Poe had the misfortune to have as his literary executor a man who believed the worst of him. Rufus Griswold was a prominent anthologist of the period. He made it his business to collect the biographical facts about each new writer of promise who appeared. When he came to write Poe's biography, he filled it with violent distortions and exaggerations, picturing Poe as a drunkard, accepting as truth all the stories of debauchery, and disregarding Poe's long years of hard, sober work. For example, Poe's early biographers, following Griswold's lead, could not make sense of Poe's military career. It was not until 1884, at the order of the President of the United States, that the army files were fully searched and the full story of Poe's enlistment became known.

Poe was a difficult, complex individual. He was a literary genius unparalleled in American history, an artist of great cunning and skill, with a marvelous imagination that tended increasingly to gloomy despair, sepulchral thoughts and grim fantasies. The full strength of his genius was devoted to his poetry, to lovely lyrics like "To Helen" or the fitful brilliance and strangeness of "The Raven." His prose seems hurried and careless, with a strong, scratchy style, deliberately roughened and rarely possessing the polished quality of Hawthorne's prose. Many of Poe's stories, like *William Wilson*, are really outlines for novels. This story, for example, is an autobiographical account of Poe's childhood in an English school,

with pages devoted to the school itself, haunting and suggestive passages, and the climax of the story, covering years of
action, disposed of in a single page. Much that Poe wrote
shows plainly the desperate effort to bring the story to an
end in time to meet a deadline for publication. And in all his
prose, the accomplishment is suggestive rather than final. He
created moods and impressions rather than narratives of action
or dramatic scenes that revealed character. Those moods, too,
were often only of one kind, somber depths of melancholy,
scenes of decay and ruin, a sad winter of the spirit, with no
indication whatever that Poe possessed the ability to range
into sunlight and warmth.

Poe was a great original, the greatest innovator in American literature. He invented the modern detective story and
was the first writer of science fiction. Stories like *The Descent
into the Maelstrom*, *The Narrative of Arthur Gordon Pym*
and *The Adventures of Hans Pfaal*, dealing with a voyage to
the moon, set the pattern for tales of fantastic adventure supported by scientific facts that science fiction writers have followed ever since. In these tales, Poe seemed to be trying to
push his imagination to the very limit of what the reader
would accept, to see how far he could go, rather than to tell a
story with some concrete purpose in mind.

Consequently, Poe's fiction most often seems to be a
demonstration of genius rather than an example of the em-
ployment of genius in a cause worthy of his gifts. He felt that
the human mind was the most wonderful of God's creations,
and by the strength of his own passionate belief in intelligence, he carried the reader along with him over any and all
improbabilities. The terrible tragedies of his life—his quarrels
with his guardian, the tragic fates of his foster mother, his
brother, his sister and his wife, and his own mysterious end

at the age of forty—made a fair estimate of him almost impossible in his own period of history. Sometimes he seemed to his contemporaries like Hawthorne's Ethan Brand, who had mastered knowledge at the expense of human sympathy, and found the unpardonable sin in the coldness of his own heart.

But today Poe seems to be a man who was fascinated by the operations of the human intellect, and unparalleled in his ability to fathom many aspects of it. His greatest stories are intellectual feats, akin to record-breaking races; he was, in many senses, a mental athlete. His last important book, *Eureka*, published in 1847, was a philosophical speculation on the nature of atomic energy. In his own time and for many years afterward, Poe's reflections on the atom were considered a hodgepodge of half-assimilated science, the wild raving of a brilliant but weakened and disordered mind. But after the discoveries of modern nuclear physicists and the development of atomic power, philosophers turned back to Edgar Allan Poe's *Eureka* with renewed respect for his clairvoyant insight and the prophetic power of his extraordinary mind.

Ralph Waldo Emerson
ॐ 1803-1882 ॐ

Henry David Thoreau
ॐ 1817-1862 ॐ

Ralph Waldo Emerson

ℰ 1803-1882 ℰ

Henry David Thoreau

ℰ 1817-1862 ℰ

CONCORD'S PHILOSOPHER AND NATURALIST

Rᴀʟᴘʜ Wᴀʟᴅᴏ Eᴍᴇʀsᴏɴ bought a small farm in Concord, Massachusetts, in 1835, for which he paid $3,500. The house was a plain, handsome dwelling set in a grove of pine trees, with tall chestnuts in the yard. There was a yellow barn behind the house and a half-acre garden full of roses and hollyhocks. Beyond these lay pastures sloping toward the Concord River.

"When I bought my farm," Emerson said, "I did not know what a bargain I had in the bluebirds, bobolinks and thrushes which were not charged in the bill. As little did I guess what sublime mornings and sunsets I was buying, what reaches of landscapes, and what fields and lanes for a tramp. . . . Still less did I know what good and true neighbors I was buying, men of thought and virtue. . . . I did not know what groups of interesting schoolboys and fair schoolgirls would greet me on the highway, and take hold of one's heart at the school exhibitions."

Emerson remained in his Concord home until his death in 1882. In all his writing about the village there is a sense of wonder and gratitude at the ceaseless appeal of its quiet life. The greatest American philosopher, who considered a day "a sound and solid good," bought his Concord home when he was thirty-two years old. He had passed through periods of darkness—extreme poverty in his youth; illness after graduation from Harvard; the death of his young wife soon after he began to preach; the loss of his two brilliant brothers, who were considered the most promising of the family; differences with his Boston congregation that resulted in his leaving the ministry. Now he had married for the second time, his life was stabilized, and there was a wonderful quality of relaxation in the happiness he found in Concord.

During the forty-three years he lived in his farmhouse, he gradually became, in the words of the great educator Horace Mann, "the most potent intellectual force on the continent." In all these years, in terms of action, Emerson did very little. A year after he settled in Concord he published a brief book of essays, entitled *Nature*. Emerson had written them previously in the Old Manse in Concord, the house that Hawthorne immortalized in *Mosses of an Old Manse*. Emerson's grandfather had been the minister at Concord and from the windows of the Old Manse had watched the beginning of the Revolution in the battle of Concord Bridge. Emerson's great influence began with a course of lectures that he delivered in Boston, about the time he made Concord his permanent residence. They aroused an extraordinary response. His listeners felt that Emerson had discovered the laws of human nature in the way that Newton had discovered laws of mathematics.

It is difficult to say what there is in Emerson's writing

that evoked this feeling. He talked about great historical figures, about poetry, Shakespeare, self-reliance, compensation, history, modern times, and these miscellaneous topics became more potent than the most inflammatory of battle cries. When Emerson's ideas are paraphrased, they are apt to seem, like the ideas of many philosophers, something everybody already knows. He has never been recognized by philosophers as an original thinker, though he has always been known as a highly original figure in the way in which his thought was expressed. At the heart of Emerson's philosophy there is a belief in intuition and a distrust in systems of philosophy and bodies of doctrine. "A man contains all that is needful to his government within himself," he wrote in his journal. Truth is discovered by intuition. There is a correspondence between the soul of man and everything that exists in the world—or, more exactly, between the soul of man and everything that is known to man. The purpose of life is to acquaint man with himself: God is within each man, and all real good or evil that can befall him must be from himself. As we are born with a God-given moral sense, our lives are shaped by the ideals we form: "All things are moral; the perogative of man is to feel this infinity within him and make himself its willing instrument."

Placing the center of existence in intuition led to the school of New England philosophy known as Transcendentalism, the individual's own inner light guiding his conduct and his perception of truth. Transcendentalism led many New England thinkers and poets to extraordinary behavior as they followed the promptings of the inner light. At one extreme there were colonies like Brook Farm that were started to blaze the way for a reformation of mankind. At the other extreme there were solitary philosophers like Henry David Thoreau, who for a short while retired to a cabin in the woods and had as little as possible to do with organized society.

Emerson himself never accepted Transcendentalism. He refused to be bound by any system of doctrine, saying that he wanted to feel free to say what he felt and thought and recognizing that later he might feel differently. This seems to leave everything at the mercy of change, but Emerson did not mean that he wished to be free of responsibility: the same moral sense would be operating in his future views as in those he held at the moment. The faith in intuition that sent others skittering off in eccentric conduct was controlled by his strong religious sense, his profound learning and his personal warmth. It enabled him to make of a nebulous core of belief a strong and positive code of life.

So his lectures, delivered with quiet earnestness, tranquil humor and superb poetic imagery, held his listeners spellbound. He seemed to them a man who possessed some secret —"the secret of a deeper, freer, more harmonious life." They received from Emerson a more hopeful and optimistic view of life, greater confidence in themselves and greater courage in facing the world. Compared with his contemporaries, Emerson published relatively little: *Poems* in 1841, the famous *Essays* in two series in 1841 and 1844, *Representative Men* in 1850, *English Traits* in 1856, *The Conduct of Life* in 1860 and *Society and Solitude* ten years later.

His lecture tours took him to England in 1848 and as far west as San Francisco in 1871. Throughout his life people made their way to his home to listen to the Sage of Concord and to seek his advice. Almost all the great New England writers were influenced, assisted or taught by Emerson, but the most famous of his followers was a Concord boy named Henry David Thoreau.

Not far from Concord, beside Walden Pond, Thoreau built one of the most famous houses ever erected. It was a cabin ten feet wide and fifteen feet long, and Thoreau built it at a cost of $28.12½. Here he went in the summer of 1845, not to live cheaply nor to live dearly, as he said, but to transact some private business with the fewest obstacles. The result was *Walden*, one of the most original books in American literature.

Henry Thoreau was born in Concord on July 12, 1817. He was a strong, dark-haired boy of medium height with such an owlish air of solemnity that the Concord boys called him The Judge.

Henry grew up in a quiet, hard-working family, with one older brother and an older and a younger sister. Several maiden aunts lived in the same home and kept a watchful eye on the progress of the youngsters. From his earliest years, Henry loved the woods. He lived out of the house as much as possible, but he did not like sports or games, preferring to hunt, skate or fish or simply to tramp along the Concord River.

His favorite haunt was Walden Pond. This was a deep, well-like lake, with no visible inlet or outlet, half a mile wide and a mile and three-quarters in circumference. The water was always cold and remarkably transparent. By popular report, the lake was bottomless. One of its singular characteristics was that it was higher in dry periods than during rainy seasons.

Walden was completely surrounded by hills covered with dense growths of pine and oak, and these woods were a favorite hiding place of runaway slaves during the days of the Underground Railway. As a boy, Henry enjoyed fishing on Walden Pond with a companion on summer nights. They would first build a fire on the water's edge because they believed it attracted the fish. When they stopped fishing, late at night, they would throw the burning brands from their fire high in the air, like skyrockets, until they descended to the lake to be quenched with a loud hiss, leaving total darkness around.

Henry went to school at Concord Academy and won a scholarship to Harvard. His sisters and aunts helped pay his college expenses. He worked hard and quietly at college, getting good marks and teaching school between terms. He walked about the campus with his head down, as if looking for tracks in the woods. He had very little to say and became known at Harvard as the student who was half graduate and half Algonquin.

After he was graduated, he taught at Concord Academy with his brother John. According to Concord tradition, John was the more gifted of the brothers, and only his early death prevented him from becoming famous. Henry, unlike John, disliked society and all regular routines of life. He worked hard and skillfully, was a good carpenter, pencil maker, cabinetmaker and farm hand, as well as a good surveyor and a good schoolteacher, though considered too lenient because he would never punish the students. Moreover, he honestly could not see why so much work was necessary in this world. With his simple tastes, he found he could labor a few days making pencils and so earn enough to keep himself in all essentials for months. He wrote irregularly, kept a journal, and when Ralph Waldo Emerson settled in Concord, Henry became an occasional visitor at the meetings of the Transcendental Club.

During vacations or in periods between his jobs, Henry walked over much of New England. He could walk thirty miles a day, day after day. Both Henry and his brother had fallen in love with the same girl, Ellen Sewall, who did not live in Concord. Both considered themselves engaged to her. Whatever the truth of the story, the legend is that each brother, finding the other in love with Ellen, tried to give way to the other. Her family did not approve of either of them, and she married someone else. They did not quarrel over her. About the time of their mixed-up romance, they set out on the expedition that gave Henry the material for his famous book *A Week on the Concord and Merrimack Rivers*.

They set out on the evening of August 31, 1839, in a fifteen-foot boat they had built in a week. They loaded it with potatoes and watermelons, carried a tent, and used buffalo skins for a bed. They floated down the Concord, watching the fish, birds and tortoises, camped at night on a hillside, while foxes rustled in the leaves around them and owls hooted in the trees. Crossing to the Merrimack River by a canal, they began rowing against or floating with the current, sailing before the wind, talking with lock keepers on the canals and with canal boatmen on the river. Nothing very striking happened on their trip. Yet, at a time when Yankee sailors were making tremendous voyages to the Far East, and travelers everywhere were penetrating unknown lands and writing books about them, it was genius that enabled Henry Thoreau to make a week's trip in a rowboat more interesting than a cruise around the world.

For two years, Thoreau lived with the Emersons in Concord. He took care of the grounds and garden, was a familiar family friend, and wrote articles on nature for *The Dial*. Aside from his walking trips and a brief stay in New York, where he served as a tutor in the home of Emerson's brother, Thoreau rarely left Concord.

More and more he had come to the conclusion that much of the work done in the world is unnecessary. "I am convinced," he wrote, "both by faith and experience, that to maintain one's self on this earth is not a hardship but a pastime, if we live simply and wisely." Near the end of March, 1845, to test his belief, Henry borrowed an ax and on a hill above a crescent-shaped cove of Walden cut down some tall straight pines to build his wilderness cabin. Emerson had bought the land not long before. On July 4, 1845, Thoreau moved into his house. He planted two acres of beans, potatoes, corn, peas and turnips, and on an impulse also planted a long series of rows of pine trees. They grew to great height and eventually became a long symmetrical row of columns in the woods, one of the landmarks of Concord.

Every morning, Henry said, brought him a cheerful invitation from nature to make his life simple. He arose early, bathed in the pond, ate breakfast, and sat in the sun in his doorway, watching the birds that were singing or noiselessly flitting in the bushes. He was constantly absorbed in the spectacle of the wealth of nature. He decided that people ought to work one day a week and rest six. He lived well on vegetables, wild strawberries, blackberries, fish, only purchasing necessities like sugar, salt and bacon. Blackberries and blueberries grew in abundance at his front door, bees buzzed in the flowers, fish jumped and splashed in the lake, a mink slipped silently down to the shore while he watched, and his bean patch flourished so richly that he sold the excess over his needs for $16.94.

During the first fourteen months of his stay at Walden, his expenses came to only $8.76. During his second summer he planted a smaller garden, feeling he had profited too much from the first. He left Walden permanently on September 6, 1847, two years, two months and two days from the time he moved into his cabin. He felt he had shown that a simple life could be lived inexpensively, but he was careful to advise his readers not to try to follow his example unless they were really prepared to do so.

Thoreau opposed the Mexican War and did not approve of slavery. He refused to pay his poll tax ($1.50) as a matter of principle, believing it wrong for an individual to contribute to the support of governments whose policies were morally wrong. As a result, he was confined in the Concord jail. His cell mate was a man arrested for barn-burning. There is a story that Emerson passed by and seeing his friend behind bars asked him what he was doing in there. Thoreau replied, "What are you doing out there?"

His two great books, *Walden* and *A Week on the Concord and Merrimack Rivers,* had been largely written during his stay in his cabin on the lake. More exactly, *A Week* was rewritten there, for Henry built the book from extracts from his journal, and had published sections of it in *The Dial* several years before. Several publishers rejected the book. Early in 1849 it was brought out by the firms of Munro in Boston and Putnam's in New York. An advertisement in the volume announced that *Walden*, by the same author, was soon to appear. However, *A Week* sold only two hundred and fifteen copies, and *Walden* did not appear until 1854. After Henry became famous, another edition of *A Week on the Concord and Merrimack Rivers* was brought out in 1862; and by an oversight the advertisement saying that *Walden* was soon to appear was left in it, though the book had been published eight years before. Both have since been republished many times, and are among the most widely read of all American classics, with more than one hundred and fifty editions listed for *Walden* alone.

The few years that were left to him were years of slowly increasing recognition.

Thoreau made three trips to Cape Cod, visited Canada, and traveled as far west as Minnesota. As *Walden* made Concord famous, the villagers forgot their old hostility and appointed him surveyor-in-chief of the town. He died on May 6, 1862, and was buried in Sleepy Hollow beside his brother.

With the years, his writing became influential. His essay on civil disobedience helped form the view of Tolstoy in Russia and Gandhi in India, becoming the cornerstone of Gandhi's passive resistance policy. Consequently, some critics believe that Thoreau is the most influential writer America ever produced.

But it is as a naturalist and as a writer of memorable phrases and passages that Thoreau is known at home. "Time is but the stream I go a-fishing in," he wrote in the chapter of *Walden* called "Where I Lived, and What I Lived For." "I drink at it; but while I drink I see the sandy bottom and detect how shallow it is. Its thin current slides away, but eternity remains. I would drink deeper; fish in the sky, whose bottom is pebbly with stars." These passages are as numerous in Thoreau's prose as the blueberries that grew around his cabin. They leap out of the pages unexpectedly, in the midst of the most commonplace observations. Writing of food, he will suddenly say: "Our whole life is startlingly moral. There is never an instant's truce between virtue and vice. Goodness is the only instrument that never fails. In the music of the harp which trembles round the world it is the insisting upon this which thrills us."

84

"Our village life would stagnate," Thoreau wrote, "if it were not for the unexplored forest and meadows which surround it. We need the tonic of wildness . . . We can never have enough of nature." He tended often to preach his own love of nature in sentences as gnarled as the roots of a tree. His love of paradox and his elliptical phrases frequently gave a crabbed effect to his most eloquent passages. Yet at his best, as in the magnificent chapter on woodland sounds in *Walden*, he is unequaled among nature writers. Poetry gleams through passages like that describing the coming of spring to Walden Pond—poetry as rare and strange as the play of a nighthawk that he saw tumbling and sporting in the air, showing the underside of its wings that gleamed like a satin ribbon in the sun. His sharpest observations, polished to diamondlike brilliance, are combined with a matter-of-fact ordinariness in which he disclaims anything more than an average man's view of things. When he came to sum up the meaning of his years at Walden Pond, he merely said, "I learned this, at least, by my experiment, that if one advances confidently in the direction of his dreams, and endeavours to live the life which he has imagined, he will meet with a success unexpected in common hours."

Emerson outlived his young friend by twenty years. He continued to live quietly in Concord, weaving the net of associations that were as much a part of his philosophy as the words he put on paper. The goodness of his life became legendary: he was a loving husband, a wise and tender father, a good neighbor, a useful citizen in all his works. Almost the only noteworthy event of his life in the sense of excitement came when his house burned to the ground. His neighbors saved his books and papers, one Concord townsman remaining in the garret and handing out papers until the roof fell in. A subscription then raised $5,000 to rebuild the house. As Emerson was already an elderly man, and had been weakened by exposure during the night spent in fighting the flames, another subscription raised $11,000 to send him abroad to recover his health.

In his later years Emerson came to be regarded as an inspirational writer rather than as an original thinker. His philosophical works were disparaged because they could not be organized into a unified system of philosophy akin to the systems of the great European thinkers. Emerson was valued as a fine poet and teacher, as a writer of intuitive genius who possessed a unique faculty of finding illustrations for his most profound thoughts in common things, and at the same time investing common experience with profound meaning. So his essays seemed to possess glancing observations of truth rather than an organic body of thought. They were filled with the play of his mind, as brilliant as the play of sunshine on the surface of a rushing stream, and it was almost as difficult to codify his message as it would be to codify the meaning of the flickering lights and shadows on the stream.

A great part of his thought was devoted to everyday matters that are seldom found in the works of philosophers. He greatly admired the opinions on world politics of one of his neighbors, a farmer named Edmund Hosmer, and carefully published them in *The Dial*. To an extraordinary extent, Emerson used the full resources of his tremendous intellect and his profound range of learning—Oriental philosophy or Greek and Latin literature—when he was discussing simple matters at home. On the other hand, when he discussed intellectual matters, he used the plainest of illustrations—weeds and nettles, clearing land, matters that anyone could understand.

The unity of his philosophy was to be found in the harmony of his life with his writing. Other philosophers can be studied with their work apart from their daily life, but not Emerson. Other philosophers created towering structures of thought, organized in all details, to explain the relation of man and the universe, but in their own daily life were men of their time. For Emerson, the way he lived in Concord was as much a part of his life work as the words he put on paper. The sky-blue river and the river-blue sky, the wood lots and old roads, the wild orchards and the granite rocks, the fabric of common life that he wove with his friends and neighbors, all fused into a unity in Emerson's work as in the work of no other American writer. "It was good to meet him in the wood-paths," wrote Nathaniel Hawthorne, "with that pure intellectual gleam diffused about his presence . . . encountering each man alive as if expecting to receive more than he would impart. It was impossible to dwell in his vicinity without inhaling more or less the mountain atmosphere of his lofty thought."

Herman Melville

 1819-1891

Herman Melville

EPIC OF THE SEA

 1819-1891

THE DATE WAS June 5, 1839. The ship was the packet *St. Lawrence*, bound for Liverpool from New York. A young seaman named Herman Melville (incorrectly called Norman Melville on the crew list) had all the symptoms of seasickness while the *St. Lawrence* was still tied up at Pier 14 on the East River.

As he went aboard ship, he was weak, dizzy and almost blind. He stretched out on a coil of chain cable and slept. When he awakened he returned to the dock and lingered until after darkness fell before going aboard the ship again. When the *St. Lawrence* set out to sea, he was still sick, and seasickness added to his misery. The first time he was sent aloft he climbed to the top of the mast in the darkness and held on, for the waves around the ship looked to him like cliffs about ready to fall in upon him.

But on the second day out, after he had scrubbed decks, cleaned the chicken coop and the pigpen, he suddenly felt fine. With all sails set, the ship "gave a sort of bound like a horse. She went plunging along, shaking off the foam from her bows . . . And I felt a wild exulting in my own heart, and felt as if I would be glad to bound along so around the world."

So began the seafaring career of Herman Melville, one of the most powerful of American novelists, whose work was to culminate in his tremendous sea story, *Moby-Dick*, twelve years later.

Herman Melville was born in New York on August 1, 1819, the son of an imaginative, romantic, but generally unsuccessful merchant and importer. His mother was the daughter of General Peter Gansevoort, a famous Revolutionary patriot who had played a part in the defeat of Burgoyne. His father's father was Major Thomas Melville, who participated in the Boston Tea Party.

Herman Melville was an active, energetic boy who grew up in New York and Albany, moving from one place to the other with the rise and fall of the family fortunes. When they prospered, they lived in New York, and when they did not, they lived in Albany under the bounty of General Gansevoort. Mr. Melville loved his family, and his wife loved him with undiminished affection, but he was a wildly impractical business man, borrowing increasingly large amounts from his father-in-law (sometimes many thousands of dollars a year), traveling much in Europe, looking up titled relatives in Scotland, telling his children vivid stories of his adventures, and, upon his death in 1832, leaving his widow heavily in debt, with her inheritance from her father exhausted by her husband's borrowings against it.

Herman Melville was the best student at Albany Academy. After his father's death he was employed in an Albany bank and later in his brother's fur business. At fifteen, he worked on his uncle's farm near Pittsfield, Massachusetts. His uncle had been a great international banker in Paris before the

French Revolution, and still had the elegant manner of the court of Louis XVI as he worked in the hayfields. At eighteen, Herman taught school near Pittsfield, and at twenty, he sailed on his first voyage on the *St. Lawrence*.

When the ship reached Liverpool, Herman set out, carrying his father's guidebook, to retrace his father's footsteps about the city. But Liverpool had grown so fast the old landmarks were gone. Herman was disappointed, but the experience gave him some adventures that he related with quizzical humor in *Redburne* several years later.

Soon after his return to the United States, Herman sailed on the *Acushnet* on a whaling voyage to the Pacific. For a year and a half he remained on the ship, but on July 9, 1842, at the island of Nukehiva in the South Seas, the harsh routine of the whaleship and the unbroken perspective of the long voyage ahead proved too much for him, and he deserted. With him was a shipmate his own age, Tobias Greene. The natives received them with much interest and friendliness, probably, Herman suspected, because they intended to eat them later.

Consequently, there was always an undercurrent of uneasiness in Herman's enjoyment of the idyllic island life and the playful attention of the lovely native girls. When a French ship appeared, Toby Greene hurried to it for help and never came back. Increasingly uneasy, Herman soon made his escape. Precisely what happened will never be known. Herman reached Boston two years later, in October, 1844. During these years he had been rescued, involved in a mutiny, arrested, jailed and burdened with handcuffs; he had escaped, lived on plantations and islands, worked as a clerk in Honolulu, and served in the United States Navy. Fact and fiction became permanently intermingled, for as soon as he landed, he wrote *Typee* (1846), dealing with his island adventures and his life among the cannibals. As it became sensationally popular, he followed it with *Omoo* (1847), which made him a celebrity in both England and America. Many people said the books were fabrications; some writers insisted there was no such person as Herman Melville; but by and large the books were read with interest. Longfellow enjoyed them; Hawthorne reviewed Melville's work favorably; Walt Whitman wrote an article praising them but also cautioning Melville about his flippancy—a criticism the books deserved. Suddenly Toby Greene appeared. He had read *Typee*, and said it was all true. But he had not run away and left Herman with the cannibals—the French ship had sailed with him aboard against his will. Toby later became a journalist and editor, named his first child after Melville, and during the Civil War served as a clerk in the headquarters of General Grant.

At twenty-six, Herman was a celebrity, but he was also something of a target for jokes as the man who had lived among the cannibals. When he married Elizabeth Shaw, of Boston, a newspaper article protested that it was not fair to the sweetheart he had left in the islands. But Melville considered himself a fortunate man on his wedding day. His bride was a charming woman and the daughter of the chief justice of Massachusetts. He also found a four-leaf clover on the morning he was married.

Having written two factual narratives that were believed to be romances, Melville said he was now going to write a romance, expecting it would be taken for fact. The result was *Mardi*. This novel disappointed his readers, and the critics were severe. They said that Melville had won a reputation and was trying to live up to it.

The opposite was true. Melville was trying to live down his reputation; he wanted to be known as a serious writer, not as somebody who had known a lot of cannibals. His next book was *Redburne*, a thinly disguised account of his first voyage on the *St. Lawrence*, one of his happiest books, a tale of the sea written before his sea stories were made to carry a burden of cosmic significance. Next came *White-Jacket*, dealing with the life of a common seaman in the navy. In five years Melville had written five books. Three of them were successful, two of them sensationally so. But Melville was tired. He needed a rest, a change of scene, a new inspiration. With $2,050 borrowed from his father-in-law, he bought Arrowhead, the old Melville farm near Pittsfield, where he had worked as a boy. There he was happy—"I have been plowing and sowing and raising and painting and praying," he wrote—and there he planned his epic of the sea.

To be the kind of book he wanted to make it, *Moby-Dick*, which appeared in 1851, should have been a life work, slowly organized and shaped. But there was no time permitted him. His earlier novels had been popular, but he had earned very little from them, not nearly enough to support his growing family. His concept of *Moby-Dick* was majestic, and he was at the height of his power as a writer of the sea. But he was forced to work under terrific pressure. He sat at his desk all day, not even stopping to eat. At night he rode into the village for relaxation and the next morning rose early to begin writing. The printing of *Moby-Dick* began long before he had finished it. Thus he was unable to change the early sections when different ideas came to him near the end, and the novel hardened into a permanent mold as material had to be added to make the later part conform with the first. He was under a constant strain to keep up with the printer's demand for copy and felt that his brains were being ground down, day after day.

In this fashion he wrote the strange story of the possessed and implacable Captain Ahab, scouring the seas in search of a monstrous white whale. Much of the book is a direct and telling account of such experiences as he had known on the *Acushnet*. Part of the book is a compound of folklore, tales of shipwreck, accounts of whales in poetry and legends, discussions of ambergris and everything else remotely connected with whales. Still another element in *Moby-Dick* is the singular Shakespearean dialog, in which the characters talk like people in Elizabethan drama. Much of the book is written in a violent exclamatory prose, with vehement and not altogether convincing addresses from the author to the reader. The total effect is often formless and chaotic, that of a mysterious and tragic experience undergone by people who, for some reason, speak in stilted and wooden phrases, to the accompaniment of a plunging and impassioned tirade by the author.

Yet the apparent formlessness of the book is part of its grand design and contributes to the unforgettable impression of the sea that it communicates. The "great shroud of the sea" was always present in Melville's mind as James Fenimore Cooper was always conscious of the immensity of the forest. The story surges and storms inexplicably, drifts in calm and dullness, and is swept on wildly into its climax in tragedy, in a sea-pattern of constant change and monotony. Melville had attempted to write an epic, and the epic sweep of the story depended on the contrast of ocean and men, on the pursuit through the depths of the white whale, as a symbol of evil, like the dragon in the old Northern sagas. And when, at the end, the white whale crushes the ship and the great shroud of the sea rolls over it, the apparent formlessness of Melville's story is justified by the power of the effect he produced, a story that seems part of the ocean itself.

"What a book!" exclaimed Nathaniel Hawthorne. There were many readers in Melville's own time who were able to appreciate the unique quality of *Moby-Dick*, but in general it was received with derision and was described as a frenzy of invention, rant and raving. Melville was only thirty-two years old. He had been writing for six years and had produced six novels. He was exhausted, but he was not yet able to get his bearings. In a mood of bitter disappointment, he wrote *Pierre* (1852), a confused, disorderly, psychological study of a writer whose fate bore some resemblance to his own. "The craziest fiction extant," said one review, which was typical of many. In 1854, Melville published *Israel Potter*, a story of Revolutionary days, with bright and amusing passages, but plainly showing the effects of fatigue, and characterized by a plodding literalness rather than by inspiration. *Piazza Tales* (1856) contained at least one masterpiece, *Benito Cereno*, the story of slaves who capture a ship and hold the officers captive because they cannot navigate it.

In 1856, Melville went abroad to rest. Nearly thirty-eight, he had the air, the manner and something of the outlook of an elderly man. He sailed to Constantinople, where he lived at the Hotel du Globe. A passage in his journal suggests that he may have intended to stay in Constantinople a long time. But the city of 1,500,000 was dangerous; as Melville wandered around alone, he noted in his journal: "a terrible place to be robbed or murdered in." When he became completely lost in the narrow streets, he realized that it was like being lost in the woods—"No names on the streets. No numbers—no anything." The rotten and wicked-looking houses were so gloomy it seemed to him "as if a suicide hung from each rafter within."

He left Constantinople and visited Egypt, with a sensation of awe and terror coming over him at the sight of the pyramids: nothing in nature gave an idea of such vastness. With only one day to spend at the site, he started at two o'clock the next morning over the desert to Jerusalem. The first part of the trip was dangerous, and the guide hurried him on, in intense darkness after the moon set, to reach the mountains before dawn. Exploring the hills around Jerusalem, and studying "the plague-stricken splendor" of the ancient temples, then traveling slowly alone through Europe, Melville spent seven months abroad. When he returned to the United States in 1857, he told his family that he was not going to write any more. He lectured briefly on his travels, sold his Pittsfield farm, and settled in New York, where he became an official in the custom service.

He remained in the service for nineteen years. Gradually his name was all but forgotten. During the Civil War he wrote a number of very fine war poems and a long poem on the Holy Land, "Clarel." It was not published until 1924. Shortly before Melville's death, which occurred in 1891, he published *Billy Budd*, another work on his familiar theme of the struggle of authority on shipboard, but written with an artistry that the hurried pace of his early writings had never permitted.

There have been few cases in which a great writer's name was so completely obliterated as Melville's. Aside from his friendship with Hawthorne, to whom he dedicated *Moby-Dick*, he was on intimate terms with few other writers. The public that had enjoyed his early adventure stories did not like the profound depths of his greater books. His work at the Custom House and his family occupied him, and after the death of his oldest son, Malcolm, in 1867, he seldom went out in public. One other son, who died in 1886, and two daughters, who lived until 1934 and 1938, comprised his family.

The rediscovery of Melville's work began after 1921, when Professor Raymond Weaver published a biography of him. Interest in Melville grew steadily. Many phases of Melville's life and writing were studied. Russian scholars displayed an interest that resulted in a microscopic examination of aspects of his career. Although it sometimes seems that Melville was not so great a writer as his admirers claim—or that no one could possibly be so great a novelist as his admirers insist Melville was—still, there is no question but that Melville deserved a higher rank than his long years of obscurity suggested. The quality of mystery in his work is found also in his life, and he remains a puzzling and undefined figure, despite the new information that has been unearthed.

Francis Parkman

1823-1893

Francis Parkman

HISTORIAN OF THE WILDERNESS

 1823-1893

ALMOST three hundred years passed between Columbus' discovery of the New World and the founding of the American republic. In these centuries there was little change in the life that was lived over most of the continent of North America. The Spanish, the English, the Dutch and the French sent out exploring parties, established settlements, and struggled for strategic points that would give them control of vital areas. Some of the greatest soldiers and organizers of Europe planned these ventures. Immense sums were spent on them. The greatest honors that kings had the power to bestow were held out to those who were successful. Yet through the centuries—for a far longer time than the republic has been established—very little was accomplished, and only along the eastern seaboard had the land been cleared and settled.

Thoughts like these occupied the mind of Francis Parkman. In his imagination he could see that beyond the settlements there was always the forest, gloomy and forbidding, encumbered with rocks and logs, tangled with roots and underbrush, damp with perpetual shade and redolent of decayed leaves and moldering wood. There seemed to Francis Parkman one great story that no one had tried to tell—"the history of the American forest, for this was the light in which I regarded it." Once this idea occurred to him, he said, "I was haunted with wilderness images night and day."

Francis Parkman was eighteen years old when he first conceived the idea of writing a factual narrative of the conquest of the wilderness. Knowing that the subject was entirely untouched, that no writer had approached it, that there were no reliable Indian records and that the early official accounts were hidden in the archives of European governments, he decided he must pursue his project but keep it secret. Meanwhile, he spent his vacations traveling to the scenes of Indian battles, or, on horseback, he followed the trails the Indians had used when they suddenly swept down upon the settlers.

Parkman was a superb horseman. It was said that he could handle any horse, tame or wild, and on his own favorite mount could perform tricks never seen outside a circus. He was also a dead shot with a rifle. Born in Boston on September 6, 1823, he was the son of a famous minister and the grandson of a wealthy merchant. Only eight miles from Boston his mother's father owned a tract of four thousand acres of wild and rocky woodland, and there Francis spent most of his time when not in Chauncey Hall School in Boston. He collected birds' eggs, snakes and insects, trapped squirrels and woodchucks, and practiced with a bow and arrow until he was skillful enough to shoot birds.

As soon as his great idea took shape in his mind, he began to keep a careful journal of his travels and his discoveries. At Harvard he devoted himself to the study of history so intently that he became one of the most accomplished scholars the University ever produced. Each vacation added a little more to his first hand knowledge: a trip to Pennsylvania, to the scene of an Indian massacre; rides in the hills of western

Massachusetts; a summer spent in Maine, where there were still Indians living in almost a wild state.

Parkman's ambition crystallized in the summer of 1841, between his sophomore and junior years in college. In 1842, his forest studies were interrupted, for he spent the summer in Italy. Knowing that many of the early explorers were missionaries, he lived in a monastery so he could gain insight into the religious training they had gone through before they set out for America.

After he was graduated from Harvard in 1844, Parkman studied law for two years, but he never practiced and probably never intended to. In the spring of 1846, he set out with his friend and classmate, Quincy Shaw, for the Western prairie. Shaw wanted to hunt buffalo. Parkman wanted to study the Indians. Traveling west some 1,700 miles, the two friends reached Independence, Missouri, shortly before the beginning of the war with Mexico. Independence was the eastern terminal point of both the Santa Fé Trail, which led into Mexican territory, and the Oregon Trail, which led over the Rockies to the Pacific Northwest. Parkman studied with interest the traders who were going to Santa Fé, and the emigrants, in their covered wagons, who were gathering to cross the Oregon Trail. This was only the third year of the Oregon Trail, but a thousand emigrants were assembled on the prairie, organizing into companies and readying their wagon trains for the trip over the plains and mountains.

On the third night after reaching Fort Laramie, in Wyoming, Francis Parkman awakened in violent pain. He seems to have contracted cholera, for he says that his disorder was the same as that which caused such heavy losses to the American army camped on the Rio Grande before the invasion of Mexico. Cholera was spread by drinking contaminated water. Its cause was not known at that time. Thousands of emigrants died of cholera while crossing the Oregon Trail. They did not know that the slow-moving prairie rivers were unsafe to drink. The disease was never found in the mountains above the Sweetwater River.

With heroic resolution, Parkman left Fort Laramie. If sufferers survived the first twenty-four hours of cholera, they generally had a fair chance of recovery. After riding through dry and desolate country, Parkman established a camp at a bend of Laramie Creek, in a grove fragrant with wild roses. A huge cottonwood tree spread its branches over his tent. While Parkman rested there, trying to recover his strength, a wandering party of eight hundred Sioux Indians camped around him. A chief named The Whirlwind had decided to go on the warpath.

Parkman still wanted to see an Indian war at first hand. But the constant feasts of the Indians that he was forced to attend made him ill again. "I could seldom walk without reeling like a drunken man," he wrote, "and when I rose from my seat upon the ground the landscape suddenly grew dim before my eyes, the trees and lodges seemed to sway to and fro, and the prairie to rise and fall like the swells of the ocean." He seemed "in a tolerably fair way to atone for my love of the prairie by resting there forever."

In his extremity, Parkman began to dream about the mountains. He felt there was a "spirit of energy" in them which would give him strength. The Indian camp moved on. The Whirlwind, with the childlike fickleness of the savage, forgot his plan to war against the Crows. Parkman rode into the mountains, seeking their spirit of energy. Through five days of wandering he was haunted by the thought of flowing streams: "I heard in fancy the plunging and gurgling of water among the shaded rocks." He camped near Horseshoe Creek, where the stream ran swiftly, clear as crystal, over a bed of white sand. Two days later, at noon, he reached Bitter Cottonwood Creek, at a point in the rapids where water birds were splashing and filling the air with cries. He stretched out on a log by the bank of the stream and watched the fish playing in the water. Suddenly he realized that he was growing stronger, almost by the hour, and even as he rested could feel his strength returning. He made camp at this remote and inaccessible point in the Western mountains until he was strong enough to proceed with confidence.

Parkman came back from his Western journey with enough knowledge to write truthfully of Indian life. He had lived for months among the Sioux and Ogilallah, knew Blackfeet and Crow and Snake Indians, and had become intimate with chiefs like The Whirlwind and Big Crow, Red Water, Eagle Feather, The Panther, The Hailstorm. He knew trappers and hunters and explorers, squaws and medicine men and the everyday life of the Indian villages. If he had found little nobility in the savages, nothing like what Cooper had imagined, and little romance in the wilderness, he had nevertheless come to understand how the Indians felt themselves to be at one with nature. He saw that while an Indian can imagine God as a Great Spirit, an all-wise and all-powerful ruler of the universe, still, "when danger threatens, when his hopes are broken, and trouble overshadows him, he is prone to turn for relief to some inferior agency, less removed from the ordinary scope of his faculties. To him all nature is instinct with mystic influence. Among these mountains not a wild beast was prowling, a bird singing, or a leaf fluttering that might not tend to direct his destiny or give warning of what was in store for him . . ."

On one occasion after another Parkman's knowledge of Indian psychology and his tact and courage saved his and Shaw's life. They rode south through the Rockies to the Santa Fé Trail and so returned to civilization. Parkman then wrote *The Oregon Trail*, published in 1849, one of the classics of the American West, a vigorous and compelling book despite the harsh, impatient tone with which it opens.

Parkman's health was shattered. The weaknesses of *The Oregon Trail* come from the fact that he wrote it while in his sickbed. His eyes had been weakened by the sunlight and by the alkali dust of the plains on the homeward journey. He had overtaxed his heart. He was too crippled by arthritis to sit on a horse. At the point where he had gathered much of his material and had learned life in the wilderness and among the Indians at first hand, he became an invalid, and his life work was not even begun.

His illness seemed to be a form of nervous exhaustion. He struggled against it with characteristic obstinacy. In 1848, he began sketching in the background for his major work by writing *The Conspiracy of Pontiac*. A superb brief historical study, the book appeared in 1851. Five years later, Parkman published his only work of fiction, *Vassal Morton*, which was a failure both with the public and as a work of art.

Illness kept him from being a soldier during the Civil War, deepening his depression and despondency. He could sleep only two or three hours a night and could no longer work more than two consecutive hours. He sat in a darkened room with his eyes bandaged, for they had become so sensitive they could not endure any light.

In this way, at a time when his condition was really pitiable, Parkman began his long, detailed history of the struggle for North America. He averaged only six lines a day. His wife and a son died while he was at work on the book. When he went to France for treatment, physicians there told him that he would become insane if he continued to write.

Parkman was forty-two years old before he began the actual composition of the work that had occupied him since he was eighteen. Under the title of *France and England in the New World*, he visualized a cycle of seven major books, running to almost 750,000 words. In outline, he was writing a chronicle of the seizure of the land from the Indians by the French, the defeat of their "effete and cumbersome feudalism" by the English and, in his last pages, the defeat of the English by the American colonists.

His purpose was to inform the American people of the struggles and heroism that had been necessary to win the continent, and to warn them against the kind of practices that had lost America for their predecessors.

His first and most difficult volume, *Pioneers of France in the New World*, reviewed the complicated relations of France and Spain, the first settlements, and traced the conflicts over the colonies to their roots in the age-old rivalries of the European monarchs.

In the early colonizing ventures, there was none of the urge to create a new world that lay behind the founding of some of the New England colonies. The early Spanish colonists wanted loot. One of the first French settlements consisted of forty convicts who were left on a desolate island near Nova Scotia. But with the coming of missionaries, the motive changed. "These men aimed at the conversion of a continent," Parkman wrote. "They surveyed a field of labor whose vastness might tire the wings of thought itself, a scene repellent and appalling, darkened with omens of peril and woe."

The epic itself really begins with the founding of Quebec

in 1608. The first great scene is that of Champlain establishing the fort "where the fierce sun fell on the bold, baking rock, with its crisped mosses and parched lichens." One after another, Parkman introduced the heroes. Champlain himself, with his matter-of-fact air, who loved the New World, "the piney odor of the forests, the noise of waters, the sharp and piercing sunlight"; Frontenac, who was fifty-two years old before he came to Canada, a ruined man, elegant, ostentatious, lavish; Père Marquette, who paddled a canoe 2,500 miles in four months; La Salle, who mastered eight Indian languages and led his handful of men from the Great Lakes to Texas. The lives of such men sustained Parkman's inspiration through twenty-seven years of writing on his subject.

Parkman traveled to Canada and Europe repeatedly to search for the original documents needed for his history. When he could not write at all, he cultivated a garden. His grandfather, the merchant, had been a fine gardener, and in following his example Parkman found a measure of peace and content. He developed several new varieties of flowers and wrote *The Book of Roses*, which became the authoritative study of the subject. For a period, he was a professor of horticulture at Harvard and was an overseer and fellow of the college. Totally blind, he envied his friend and fellow-historian William Prescott—"Confound him," Parkman said—because Prescott could at least see enough to read his proofs. But, said Parkman, "I am no better off than an owl in the twilight."

As one volume after another of Parkman's work appeared, *The Jesuits in North America* in 1867, *La Salle and the Discovery of the Great West* in 1869, *The Old Regime in Canada* in 1874, *Count Frontenac and New France* in 1877, a kind of miracle took place in Parkman's health. The completion of each volume seemed to have a bracing effect on him.

His physical condition steadily improved as the work went on. He had a fresh impetus of renewed well-being as he approached the end of twenty-seven years of labor. When he came to write, in *Montcalm and Wolfe* (1884), the last great scene of the tremendous story, the fall of Quebec to the English in 1759, Parkman was stronger than when he began.

A century and a half of hitherto unknown history had been clarified, explained and dramatized in his work, with a care that made his books the final authority. His narrative was as good as that of the famous English historian Macaulay. His scholarship equaled that of the best historians of his time. There is a tangled quality in many of Parkman's chapters, for he was breaking a path into history that had never been written before. But for the most part his writing is clear and sharp with an unfailing grasp of reality, and with scenes of excitement that communicate the freshness and wonder of the New World that were felt by the first explorers. And, throughout, the sense of the wilderness is always present, like the vision of the immensity of the ocean that pervades Melville's books.

The series ended with *Montcalm and Wolfe*. But there were blank spaces in the narrative that had not been covered. To make his work complete, Parkman wrote an additional book, *A Half-Century of Conflict*, which he completed in 1893. He died in that same year, on November 8.

In Parkman's lifetime the country had been settled from the Atlantic to the Pacific. The wilderness had been tamed. Through the three preceding centuries the continent had defeated every effort of Europe to master it. In a few decades under the American republic the whole land was occupied and settled. The forests that had seemed to the first visitors to America to be so terrifying in their solitude turned out to be sources of wealth beyond all the gold mines that lured the first explorers. The great plains that had been so forbidding in their treeless expanse yielded more food than any other land on earth. Beneath the desert sands that the conquistadors had crossed and recrossed, searching for the seven cities of Cibola, there lay fortunes in oil and minerals, and the desert itself, when irrigated, produced more wealth than all the Aztec empire.

But Francis Parkman did not believe that Americans could rest content with what had been accomplished. The task of his country, he wrote, had only begun: "She has tamed the savage continent, peopled the solitude, gathered wealth untold, waxed potent, imposing, redoubtable. And now it remains for her to prove, if she can, that the rule of the masses is consistent with the highest growth of the individual, that democracy can give the world a civilization as mature and pregnant, ideas as energetic and vitalizing, and types of manhood as lofty and strong, as any of the systems which it boasts to supplant."

Mark Twain

1835 - 1910

Mark Twain

THE HUMOR OF AMERICA

 1835-1910

SAMUEL L. CLEMENS, better known as Mark Twain, was born on March 30, 1835, at Florida, Missouri. When he was four years old, his family moved to Hannibal, Missouri, a town of 1,500 people on the banks of the Mississippi.

To Samuel Clemens the town of Hannibal was a wonderland, the center of a summer world, bright and fresh and brimming with life. It was a wonderland that consisted of four general stores, three sawmills, two hotels, a tobacco factory, a distillery and a slaughterhouse. Around Hannibal were the ubiquitous woods that surrounded all American towns, groves of sugar and rock maples, dogwood and red oak, where the boys played their endless games of pirates or Indians. The woods exercised a magnetic attraction on them. They were filled with a physical ache to be out in the open, an emotion of American boyhood which Mark Twain described perfectly, and which is never found in the novels or memoirs of English or European writers.

It seemed to him that the noon recess would never come. The air was utterly dead. There was not a breath stirring. It was the sleepiest of sleepy days. The drowsy murmur of five and twenty studying scholars soothed the soul like the spell that is in the murmur of bees. Away off in the flaming sunshine, Cardiff Hill lifted its soft green sides through the shimmering veil of heat, tinted with the purple of distance; a few birds floated on lazy wing high in the air; no other living thing was visible but some cows, and they were asleep. Tom's heart ached to be free, or else to have something of interest to do to pass the dreary time.

Everything outside the schoolroom was of ceaseless interest: the river boats passing on the Mississippi, a mile wide at this point; the piles of freight on the levee; McConnell's Cave on Holliday Hill, two miles south of town, a deep limestone cavern where an eccentric physician had once stored cannon, planning to lead an invasion to conquer Mexico.

The boys of Hannibal roamed this wonderland like inquisitive and restless animals, animated as bear cubs and noisy as squirrels, forever climbing cliffs and trees, creeping into and out of the upper floors of buildings, breaking through the underbrush with the wide-eyed air of astonishment that James Fenimore Cooper had noticed in deer and racoons. They turned everything into games. Even their chores became play. Carrying water from the town pump, they imagined they were racing supplies to a farmhouse surrounded by Indians. Their most successful games and their happiest memories were those in which their imaginary actions roughly coincided with reality, and their boyhood fancies made work easier or more interesting or funny or profitable.

Because Samuel Clemens' father died when he was twelve, he went to work early. He was a paper boy, a grocer's clerk, a blacksmith's helper, and, at twelve, a printer's devil. He built the fire, carried water, swept out the office, set type, distributed type, ran the press, washed the press, folded the papers and delivered them. Soon he began writing little jokes and stories that were printed in the paper. He even sold one story to a Boston magazine called *The Carpetbag* and another to *The Saturday Evening Post*. When his older brother, Orion, started a newspaper of his own, Sam Clemens became the printer. Orion never paid him, so he got a job with a Saint Louis paper, saved his money, and at seventeen made his way to New York.

He hated to set type, perhaps because he was a very slow typesetter. All his life he dreamed of some machine that would magically select the right letters and form the words. And he developed a ferocious hatred, often found among printers, for long sentences and for writers who said the same thing over and over.

Sam was a good printer and had no difficulty in getting work. He lived for a time in a mechanics' boardinghouse on Duane Street in New York, then moved to Philadelphia, where he worked on three different newspapers. Because Orion had started another newspaper in Iowa and needed his help, Sam went west again. His next move was to Cincinnati, where he saved his money, planning to explore the Amazon River in South America.

While he was in New Orleans, on his way to the tropics, a river-boat pilot offered to teach him piloting for $500. One hundred dollars was to be paid in cash and the remainder taken from his earnings after he became a pilot.

Sam borrowed $100 from his brother-in-law and began seventeen months of intensive study, sailing up and down the Mississippi. He was required to learn every landmark on 1,200 miles of the river. Standing beside a wheel as high as his head, in a glass-encased pilothouse high above the decks, the pilot of a Mississippi steamer was the absolute master of vessels worth as much as $250,000. Pilots had to make the decision whether to tie up during a storm or keep going. The river boats were fast, making as much as fourteen miles an hour upstream, but the current of the Mississippi was fast also, so the river boats had to hug the shore, keeping to the very edge of deep water where the current was not so strong. So they raced along, close to the very branches of the trees, their tall stacks rising above them, the glow from their fires shining over the water, the lights twinkling in the gold and white cabins—the most luxurious and spectacular and glamorous form of travel America had even known.

Sam soon became a pilot of first-class ships: the *Alonzo Child*, the *Pennsylvania*, the *Aleck Scott*. Before he was twenty-three years old, he was earning $250 a month, a salary roughly equivalent to $25,000 a year a century later.

When the Civil War began, Sam joined the Confederate army. He served very briefly, perhaps only two weeks. His brother Orion had been appointed lieutenant-governor of Nevada Territory by President Lincoln, and Sam set out with Orion across the prairie.

In twenty days of hard driving their stagecoach reached Carson City, the Nevada capital. Sam headed for the newly discovered gold fields, found no gold, and in 1862 became a reporter on the Virginia City *Territorial Enterprise*. He signed his articles Mark Twain, taking the name from the cry on the Mississippi river boats to indicate the depth of the water. These river boats generally needed six feet of water. When a steamer approached a bank for a landing, the leadsman measured the depth, shouting up to the pilot "mark three," meaning three fathoms or eighteen feet, then "mark twain," two fathoms or twelve feet. So Sam used the name Mark Twain, meaning safe water, go ahead or all's well.

Virginia City was then one of the richest and wildest of all Western mining towns. The streets were literally paved with low-grade gold and silver ore. The tremendous Comstock Lode, a vein of gold and silver 150 feet wide, lay directly beneath the houses. In one year, $36,000,000 was taken from the Comstock Lode. A mine that sold for $26,000 was worth $160,000,000 two years later. In all, $900,000,000 in gold and silver came out of more than 750 miles of tunnels beneath the city.

There were fifteen thousand people in Virginia City at the time Sam Clemens became Mark Twain. They were all rich or expected to be rich soon, and he noted "a glad, almost fierce intensity in every eye." He wrote in the paper of gun fights, fires, mining accidents, rackets in mine stocks, the hardships of Chinese laborers, the fate of men who became rich overnight.

In 1864 there was a sudden drop in the yield of the mines, and it was thought that they were playing out. Mark Twain went to San Francisco to sell Nevada mining stock. For a brief period he did well. Then the bottom fell out of the market. He went to work as a reporter on the San Francisco *Morning Call*, soon lost his job, and was hired by Bret Harte, then editor of a literary magazine, *The Californian*, at $12 a week.

After spending a winter in a ghost town, Mark Twain sailed in 1865 for Hawaii. The travel articles that he wrote for the Sacramento *Union* were very popular, and the paper paid him $1,000 for them. He earned another $1,500 in three weeks, lecturing about his travels. A paper paid him $1,000 to write fifty articles about a trip to New York. When he arrived in the East, a steamer, the *Quaker City*, was setting out on a six-month cruise to the Holy Land, and Mark Twain sailed along with an assignment to write articles about the trip.

His description of his companions on their way to Jerusalem seemed to the Americans of the time the funniest writing they had ever read. There was perhaps really nothing very funny in the picture of a shipload of elderly, irritable, pious, cranky and picturesque Americans, solemnly pondering over ancient ruins, swimming in the Sea of Galilee, or sneering at the Tiber because it was not so wide as the Mississippi. But Twain's account was so different from the solemn travel writing of the time, and he was so cheerfully unimpressed by the historic wonders of the Old World, that his countrymen laughed at everything he said, whether he was serious or not. The articles were made into a book, *The Innocents Abroad*, selling twelve thousand copies in one month, a hundred thousand in one year, and earning Mark Twain $1,200 to $1,500 a month.

One of the passengers on the *Quaker City* was Charles Langdon, the son of a wealthy Buffalo coaldealer whose father had sent him abroad to keep him from sowing his wild oats. He and Mark Twain became friends, and on their return Twain had dinner with Charles Langdon's family. Mark fell in love with Olivia Langdon, Charles' sister, a small, dark, delightful girl of twenty-one. But Mark was now a famous humorist, and everything he said was considered funny. In a desperate effort to appear serious and to convince Olivia that he really loved her, Mark gave up smoking. She thought that was the funniest demonstration of undying affection she had ever heard of. Next Mark gave up swearing. Still Olivia seemed not to take him seriously. Then he began to go to church. Before long he was really praying, living regularly, dressing properly, not drinking, smoking or swearing, the most solemn, upright and proper young man in the United States, which Olivia also thought was funny.

When Mark told Mr. Langdon that he wanted to marry Olivia, the old gentleman asked Mark for the names of people who had known him a long time, to whom he might write for testimonials that Mark was a man of good character. At this Mark was in trouble, for most of his friends were miners, river-boat pilots, gamblers, reporters and others whose words he suspected would not carry much weight with Mr. Langdon, and certainly wouldn't if they wrote the truth. He finally came up with five names, mostly newspaper editors and politicians, including one former governor of Nevada. They all thought it was a joke and wrote to Mr. Langdon that Mark was a complete blackguard, a scoundrel, one who should not be allowed in polite society. Mr. Langdon took the letters very seriously. He called Mark into his library. "My boy," he said, "you haven't a friend in the world. Why, I know you better than these men do, and they've known you all your life. I'll be your friend."

The marriage of Samuel Clemens and Olivia Langdon, on February 2, 1870, marked the end of his wanderings. When he returned to Buffalo after the honeymoon, Mark was worried because there had been a mix-up about where they were to live. A friend had promised to rent them an inexpensive place. To Mark's dismay, they were driven to a mansion, cheerfully lighted, far beyond his means. When they went inside, there was Mr. Langdon, who gave Mark a deed to the house—he had secretly bought it and furnished it, the Langdon family completely outfitting it even to food in the pantry.

Mark and his bride first lived in Buffalo, where Mark edited a newspaper that he had bought with Mr. Langdon. They next lived in Hartford, Connecticut, their home for seventeen years. Four children were born to them—a son who died in infancy and three daughters.

In Hartford, Mark Twain wrote his three great books:

The Adventures of Tom Sawyer, Life on the Mississippi and *Huckleberry Finn.* He wrote many others, but these were, beyond any question, his contribution to world literature. They are works of humor, but they are unlike the many other humorous books that Mark Twain wrote. The reason is that they are books about American life, and where they are funny, it is because American life is funny in the same way. Their humor is not strained or forced; it does not depend on comic exaggerations or on elaborately comic situations, but bubbles spontaneously from the truthful representation of a society that contains within it much that makes people laugh.

Mark Twain began to write *The Adventures of Tom Sawyer* in 1874. He published it during the hundredth anniversary of the Declaration of Independence in 1876. He knew that he had written a masterpiece that was sure to be popular, and at once began the sequel, *Huckleberry Finn.* But Mark Twain was also a businessman. He set aside *Huckleberry Finn* until after the success of *Tom Sawyer* should create a demand for it. Meanwhile, he busied himself promoting a patent steam generator, a new engraving process and a contraption used in carpet weaving by means of which he really expected to capture control of the carpet-weaving business of the world. He also patented a novelty scrapbook that contained a built-in mucilage folder to facilitate pasting material into it, which earned him $2,000 a year.

Many of Mr. Twain's friends were big businessmen, like Mr. Rogers, one of the founders of the Standard Oil Company. As Mark Twain clamped his cigar in his mouth and played billiards with steely concentration, he had no difficulty picturing himself as a powerful figure in American industrial life. He owned one of the first typewriters ever built and was the first author to have a telephone in his house; it connected his office with the Western Union office in Hartford. But Mark Twain's real dream of success in industry revolved around a patent typesetting machine.

A man named Paige, who worked in the Colt revolver factory, had invented a typesetter which possessed the unique faculty of almost, but not quite, working, through twelve long years. Paige had secured the financial support of a Hartford jeweler. The jeweler confided the secret of the invention to Mark Twain. Sitting in his office in his home, the genial humorist chewed thoughtfully on his cigar, knitted his bushy eyebrows, and agreed to enter the syndicate, writing out his check for $2,000 and, of course, keeping in the background.

The typesetting machine was a wonderful contraption. It had eighteen thousand moving parts, and when it was in motion, wheezing and clanking, with all eighteen thousand parts going at top speed, arms reaching out to select letters and form them into sentences, almost as fast as a human being could do it, it was worth $2,000 merely to stand by and admire the operation. However, the machine somehow selected the wrong letters, so the words came out misspelled, or did not make words at all, or, more often, only 17,999 of the moving parts moved, and the whole thing ground to a halt. The inventor possessed the natural optimism of his kind and returned undismayed to his labors, while Mark Twain put up a few more thousand dollars and returned to his billiard table, his writing desk and the lecture platform.

His daughter Olivia, then aged thirteen, started to write a book about her father. "He is the loveliest man I ever saw," she began. "Papa's favorite game is billiards, and when he is tired and wishes to rest himself he stays up all night and plays billiards."

There was no real reason why Mark Twain should have

driven himself to work so hard. Despite its humor, Olivia's observation of her father was accurate: he worked under pressure and played billiards to relax. He needed money for his business ventures. And yet his early books were terrific financial successes. *Roughing It*, dealing with his experiences in the West (1872), sold sixty-two thousand copies in four months. *The Gilded Age*, a satire on business promoters, sold forty thousand copies in two months. Mark Twain made $20,000 from *The Gilded Age* in one year and made $75,000 from *Colonel Sellers*, a play based upon it. *Life on the Mississippi* sold fifty thousand copies upon publication, and six of Mark Twain's books sold six hundred thousand copies in twelve years.

Why, then, was Mark Twain in such financial trouble? Acting on the advice of a lawyer, he had signed an unfortunate contract with a publisher which left him receiving only about $3,000 a year from his later books, despite their popularity. This arrangement seems to indicate that the publishers were the greediest as well as the most shortsighted businessmen in history. To meet the expenses of his home, and to keep his business enterprises going, Mark Twain was compelled to lecture as well as write. He was so popular on the lecture platform that he could easily earn $10,000 a year on a brief lecture tour. He hated to travel and be separated from his family, however, and the strain of lecturing to immense audiences who expected him to make them laugh every minute was increasingly difficult. His wife tried to make him give up lecturing and live on her income while he wrote his books. She had an income of from $300 to $500 a month and an inheritance of $65,000 from her father. She begged him to give up all his plans and inventions and schemes, until the time came when his writing alone would earn enough for them, since he did not want to be dependent on her money.

But Mark's business enterprises kept him so entangled that he could not do as she urged. Even before his marriage he had gone into debt for $22,000 on the Buffalo newspaper deal, and he lost $10,000 when he sold the paper.

To profit from the popularity of his books, Mark Twain organized his own publishing company. He placed in charge of it Charles Webster, the husband of his sister's daughter, a goodhearted civil engineer from Fredonia, New York. Mr. Webster's previous business experience had been managing a chalk-plate engraving company that Mark Twain also owned, and which failed.

The new publishing house was launched with *Huckleberry Finn*. The book sold thirty thousand copies at once, and within two years had sold more than any of Mark Twain's other books. Business was so good that Mark Twain drew out $40,000 in profits the first year.* But Mark Twain's other business enterprises required ever increasing amounts of money. The automatic typesetter was now costing $3,000 every month, and still did not work. All told, Mark Twain invested $190,000 in it. In 1891, when he was fifty-eight, Mark Twain was bankrupt. The publishing business failed, everything he owned was sold, his wife turned in her $65,000 to pay bills, the Hartford house was closed, and Mark Twain and his family moved abroad, where they lived for nine years. Apparently none of his business friends came to his assistance,

* Hearing that General Grant was bankrupt—his checks for household expenses were returned for insufficient funds—Mark Twain urged the ex-President to write his memoirs. A publishing house would only give Grant royalties of 10 per cent on 25,000 copies, perhaps $2,500 to $5,000. Mark Twain then published Grant's memoirs himself, giving Grant royalties of 70 per cent on each volume sold. Twain's publishing house sold 610,000 copies. The first royalty check was $200,000, the largest ever paid. Grant and his estate got $420,000 from the book. Mark Twain's publishing house earned $185,000.

for when all his assets were realized, he still owed $94,000.

Most of Mark Twain's later humorous books were written in order to make money to meet his business expenses. He was not proud of being a writer; primarily he was proud of having been a river-boat pilot, though he had some satisfaction in his business ventures when they were successful. He wrote these works hurriedly. *Roughing It* is mostly a rehash of his Western newspaper writings. When it is good, it is so because the original copy was good. But the book as a whole is inconclusive and downright dull at the end, where Twain describes his horseback rides in Hawaii. *A Tramp Abroad* (1880) was his report on a trip through Germany and Switzerland, spoofing duels, mountain climbing, yodeling and lectures on art, but not really very funny because most of what he was writing about was not funny. *A Connecticut Yankee in King Arthur's Court* (1889) is just what its title implies, and in fact the title tells the whole story. There is a good deal of slapstick in the idea of a mechanic transported back to the days of the Round Table, and getting mixed up with knights wearing hardware. But after readers grow accustomed to the novelty, the joke becomes repetitive. And the serious criticism of romantic notions of the past that are laced through the story are out of key with its burlesque.

There is none of this sort of humor in *Tom Sawyer*, *Huckleberry Finn* or *Life on the Mississippi*. Everything in *Tom Sawyer* really happened, Twain said, if not to him personally, then to boys he had known in Hannibal. The celebrated comic chapters, like those of the boys whitewashing the fence or stealing the schoolmaster's wig, may not seem so funny as they once were thought to be. The real humor of the book is in the enjoyment of life that suffuses it, not jokes, anecdotes or wisecracks, but a never failing sense of the absurd preoccupations of mankind, an acute perception of the mixture of self-importance and bewilderment with which humanity ordinarily conducts its business.

The same is true of *Huckleberry Finn*. The original of Huck was a Hannibal boy named Tom Blankenship, greatly envied by the others because he did not go to school, slept on doorsteps and empty hogsheads, and spent his time fishing and swimming—a carefree, lazy, uneducated boy, kindly and generous, who would have acted in comparable situations in the same way as Mark Twain pictured Huck Finn acting. There is a kind of final veracity in Mark Twain's writing, as if he could not essentially distort any picture, but had somehow to reflect it back as it was.

With his hatred of sham and his complete lack of affectation, the only distortion that he could permit himself in his picture of the United States was that of humor. So long as he dealt with the boy's world of Hannibal, or the river pilots, monosyllabic as Indians, navigating their stately craft, there was no real problem encountered: the books were funny because they dealt with experiences that were funny. But there was no humor in the complex plots and deals of big business, in political scandals, in the callousness of frontier society to suffering, in the exploitation of labor, and Twain's inexorable honesty would not permit him to write into something a quality that was not there.

He believed that the kind of life that was lived in Hannibal, or in thousands of American communities like it, was superior to the life that had been lived in the golden ages of the past or in wealthy and aristocratic societies of the present. He believed it to be more sensible, cleaner, kindlier, more honest, less selfish, more pleasant, more enjoyable, funnier, and truer to the essential reality of human destiny. He believed that despite much crudeness and some cruelty there lay within common American life the beginning of a really new type of civilization, that even as it stood there were points in which it was better, and that potentially there could be the growth of a free, rich and normal society such as history had never known before.

One great obstacle to that growth was the contempt or indifference of educated classes toward the values of common American life; they endorsed patterns of education that meant nothing to American children, ideas of art that meant nothing to the people at large, culture that blindly imitated the culture of the Old World. The clearest example of his feeling is in the chapter in *Huckleberry Finn* in which a Shakespearean play is produced in the village, a performance that is so affected, unreal, dishonest and tasteless that it gradually turns from a burlesque into something ghastly and horrible. Books like *A Connecticut Yankee in King Arthur's Court* or *The Prince and the Pauper* (1882) or *Personal Recollections of Joan of Arc* (1896) were intended by Mark Twain to break the hold that foreign concepts of chivalry and nobility had for many Americans, and to make them see that their own life was better, or potentially better, than the civilizations that were held up to them as models.

Mark Twain did not mean that the society he pictured was, of itself, ideal. On the contrary, he exaggerated the violence and crudeness found in it, as in the chapter about the family feud in *Huckleberry Finn* or the dull savagery of the murder in *Tom Sawyer*. Yet it had the seeds of greatness within it, and if developed along its best lines, there could be a flowering that would not be the narrow heroism of a small group, as in the days of knighthood, but would be suffused through the whole of life. The great quality of the community life of America that Mark Twain pictured lay in its warmth and humanity; in the real concern that moved the inhabitants at the trouble of their neighbors; in their common response to emergencies, in which their instinctive emotional response was uncalculating and true and good. In *Tom Sawyer*, when the children are thought to be drowned, the gloom that lies over the town is real, and when they are found to be safe, the rejoicing is tremendous. But this chapter merely builds up to a far more significant climax. When Tom and Becky Thatcher are lost for four days in the fearful depths of the cavern:

Tuesday afternoon came, and waned into twilight. The village of St. Petersburg still mourned. The lost children had not been found. Public prayers had been offered up for them, and many and many a private prayer that had the petitioner's whole heart in it; but still no good news came from the cave. The majority of the searchers had given up the quest and gone back to their daily vocations, saying it was plain the children could never be found. Mrs. Thatcher was very ill, and a great part of the time delirious. People said it was heartbreaking to hear her call her child, and raise her head and listen a whole minute at a time, then lay it wearily down again with a moan. Aunt Polly had dropped into a settled melancholy, and her gray hair had grown almost white. The village went to its rest on Tuesday night sad and forlorn.

Away in the middle of the night, a wild peal burst from the village bells, and in a moment the streets were swarming with half-clad people, who shouted, "Turn out! turn out! They're found! They're found!"

The joy in heaven that is felt when a sinner is saved seems foreshadowed by the villagers at the rescue, shouting and cheering and beating on tin pans—"nobody went to bed again," Mark Twain wrote. "It was the greatest night the little town had ever seen." His feeling about the potential greatness of such life was a profound one, and if it might be objected that the society he pictured had no great works of the spirit to show its quality, it might be answered that his own books were an example of what might be produced.

After the loss of his fortune, Mark Twain worked hard, lecturing and writing, to pay his debts. He traveled as far as Australia on lecture trips and sent back more than $2,500 to begin reducing the total amount of $94,000. He made a trip around the world and turned out a burlesque version of his own art in *Pudd'nhead Wilson* (1894), as well as many other lesser books and hasty sequels dealing with Tom Sawyer abroad, most of which are no longer read. With these and his lectures he paid off the whole debt and began to make another fortune. When he built a new home in Redding, Connecticut, in 1909, he would not enter it or have anything to do with it until it was completely finished and furnished, as was his first home with Olivia in Buffalo. His daughter Olivia died in 1896, his wife in 1904, and Mark himself died on April 21, 1910, at the age of seventy-four.

No writer in American history so summed up the spirit of the country in his time as did Mark Twain. It may even be questioned whether any great European writer expressed his own country so fully, whether Dickens spoke for all Englishmen or Balzac for all Frenchmen, in the way that Mark Twain spoke for Americans. Americans read of themselves in Mark Twain's books, saw their own boyhood reflected in Mark Twain's stories of boyhood, responded to the humor of what Mark Twain thought was funny, shared his hatred of injustice, and felt their own dimly perceived views of the world sharply outlined in his works. The range of Mark Twain's experience spanned the country, from coast to coast. He knew every part of it: sleepy Southern towns, Northern industrial communities, ghost towns in the Sierra Nevadas, mining camps and state capitals. His friends were found in every walk of life: miners, printers, river-boat pilots, ex-slaves, politicians, presidents, generals, and, in the last years of his life, kings and emperors—but principally Americans from every social level who found in Mark Twain's writing something that expressed what was most deeply American in themselves. "It was certain that a few of Mark Twain's writings were destined to live with the best in America," wrote Van Wyck Brooks, "and the man was to be remembered also as the type of his epoch, the humorist and the gambler, dramatic, shrewd, compassionate, impulsive and boyish, the 'man from Missouri' who became an American legend."

Stephen Crane

1871-1900

Stephen Crane

ACTION AND ADVENTURE

 1871-1900

STEPHEN CRANE's *The Red Badge of Courage* opens with the picture of an army resting before a battle. In the cold fog of dawn, over an amber-tinted river, there is the red, eyelike gleam of hostile campfires on the other side. The men are bewildered by a maze of rumors, as confusing as the strange countryside, and they grow increasingly nervous and quarrelsome. Everything is seen through the eyes of Henry, a boy in the 304th New York Regiment. He is preoccupied with the thought of how he will behave in battle, not precisely afraid, but uneasy because he can no longer regard himself "as a part of a vast blue demonstration."

The movement of the army is described with a marvelous clarity against its background of constant confusion. It appears that a part of the army to which the 304th New York Regiment is attached is engaged in a flank attack, moving far up the Rappahannock to fall upon the Confederate right. Perhaps the movement is timed with a frontal attack across the river, but nothing is clear, for Henry merely sees the troops moving under a dun-colored cloud of dust; experiences weariness, misery and discomfort; crosses the river by night over pontoon bridges; and finds himself rushing through another gray dawn into a sudden spatter of firing. The battle-field itself does not look like a battlefield—"it seemed a wrong place for a battlefield"—with dark lines of skirmishers in the distance, a confused impression of men floundering up a bank. Suddenly the woods burst into action, as if they had exploded, bullets whistling through the branches, twigs and leaves falling, and ahead billowing smoke filled with horizontal flashes. As the Confederates charge, the men feverishly reach for cartridges with hands that seem to be encased in invisible mittens. The young volunteer loses his concern for his own fate in a sense of being part of the regiment around him:

At last an exultant yell went along the quivering line. The firing dwindled from an uproar to a last vindictive popping. As the smoke eddied away, the youth saw that the charge had been repulsed . . . As he gazed around him, the youth felt a flash of astonishment at the blue, pure sky and the sun gleaming on the trees and fields. It was surprising that Nature had gone tranquilly on with her golden process in the midst of so much devilment.

When Stephen Crane visited the Philadelphia newspaper office where *The Red Badge of Courage* was being set up in type, editors, proofreaders, copyreaders and typesetters crowded around him to shake his hand. The book first appeared as a serial in the Philadelphia *Press* between December 3 and December 8, 1894. It was a condensed version, with eight of the twenty-four chapters eliminated, and the book reduced from fifty thousand to eighteen thousand words. The whole story was published in one issue of the New York *Press* on December 9. Thereafter it appeared in 200 small-city daily newspapers, in 250 weekly newspapers and in perhaps an additional 300 to 350 later on. At twenty-three, with no experience whatsoever in war or fighting, and with little previous experience in writing, Stephen Crane had produced one of the world's classics of war literature.

Stephen Crane was born in a red brick Methodist parsonage at No. 14 Mulberry Street in Newark, New Jersey, on November 1, 1871. His father was a well-known clergyman who possessed a distinguished literary style and wrote thoughtful books on moral and social problems, being deeply concerned "about such sins as dancing, breaking the Sabbath, reading trashy novels, playing cards, billiards and chess, and enjoying tobacco and wine, and too innocent of the world to do more than suspect the existence of greater viciousness." Stephen's father died when he was eight years old, and during his early years Stephen was helped in his education by his older brothers and sisters.

Stephen's great ambition in his boyhood was to play professional baseball. He was, in fact, a baseball player of more than average ability. At sixteen, he enrolled at Claverack Academy, a coeducational Methodist school on the Hudson River, where he was catcher on the baseball team. The boys at Claverack wore blue and gold military uniforms and drilled regularly. Stephen was a serious student, sang in the choir, became drillmaster and eventually captain of the school troop.

During vacations, Stephen lived at resort towns on the New Jersey coast, picking up news items for his brother who was the correspondent in the area for the New York *Tribune*. He entered Lafayette College, in Easton, Pennsylvania, in 1890, intending to become a mining engineer. He joined a fraternity, played baseball, boxed, played cricket, and neglected his college courses, not even bothering to turn in assignments. In January, he was asked to leave. He then enrolled at Syracuse University, where he worked regularly and led a normal college life. The following spring he made the Syracuse baseball team. He played first base, shortstop and left field, and, incredible as it seems, his biographers assert he became captain of the nine. As a baseball player he was fast and accurate, a good fielder and batter, but his throwing arm was weak, and he did not do well in center field.

While Stephen was at Syracuse he acted as correspondent for the New York *Tribune*, became a college reporter for the Syracuse newspaper and for the Detroit *Free Press*. During the summer he worked for his brother again, covering the New Jersey resorts.

After his mother's death at the end of 1891, Stephen lived in New York, where he haunted Bowery saloons and wandered through the slums, consciously gathering material for the books he intended to write. He fell in love with a well-to-do girl who encouraged his attentions. On the eve of sailing to Europe she told him that she was not merely taking a trip abroad: she had been engaged all the time she had known him and was on her way to England, where she was to marry a successful young doctor. Stephen gasped, put his hands to his face and left.

For a time, he lived with his brother's family near Paterson, New Jersey, and worked briefly for the New York *Herald* but was soon discharged. His brother hired him again to cover the resort towns on the New Jersey coast. A description that he wrote of a parade in Asbury Park of the Junior Order of United American Mechanics was misunderstood as an attack on the labor movement and Stephen was fired. His older brother also lost his job.

Stephen Crane then returned to New York, where he wrote stories, borrowed money, fell into and out of love, and, in general, behaved like any number of gifted poets, artists and musicians who have followed their careers in the city. He wrote a short novel, *Maggie: a Girl of the Streets*. No publisher would bring it out. One of his brothers loaned him

$1,000 and he published it himself.

With no experience in war, Stephen gathered the material for *The Red Badge of Courage* from a famous set of books then found in many Northern homes: *Battles and Leaders of the Civil War*. It was published in 1895, and after its popular success in the United States, *The Red Badge of Courage* became a critical success in England, and thus, somewhat reluctantly, the American critics were compelled to accept Crane. He became recognized as one of the most naturally gifted writers in American history.

One of the few natural things that Crane did after his success was to buy himself a lively little horse which he called Peanuts. He lived with his brother's family at Port Jervis, New York, hunted and fished with his nephew and nieces, and rode his horse. Crane traveled to the Far West and Mexico in 1895, in the happiest time of his life, visiting the Nebraska plains, a Nevada ranch, the Painted Desert of Arizona, loafing in New Orleans and San Antonio, and running into bandits south of the border.

Jacksonville, Florida, was headquarters for many of the groups of Cuban revolutionaries who were trying to free Cuba from Spain. With another profitable newspaper assignment, Crane went to Jacksonville, planning to sail with gunrunners who were smuggling arms into Cuba. While there, he fell in love with a woman three years older than he, Cora Taylor, or Lady Stewart, as she was in England, a New England girl who had married a British intelligence officer and had long since been separated from him. She lived in a sensationally notorious fashion in Jacksonville, perhaps too notorious to be quite believable.

Gathering material for his books, and self-conscious about his reputation as a war author who had never seen a battle, Crane sailed on the tug *Commodore*, laden with bundles of rifles and boxes of ammunition destined for Cuban rebels, in a secret mission that was the talk of Jacksonville. The *Commodore* sank in a storm. Crane went through seventy to eighty hours of exposure before he was washed up on the beach at Daytona, Florida. From this experience he wrote his second masterpiece, *The Open Boat*, but his health was so badly affected he was never again physically strong. While still convalescent, he departed for Greece to cover the war that had started between Greece and Turkey. There he saw some action, wrote a few vivid reports, and was then driven by ill-health to England. Cora Taylor, who had now become Mrs. Crane, joined him there. Crane was so lionized in London that he found it impossible to write, and the high expenses of a social life forced him to live on borrowed money despite the success of his books. The Cranes accordingly rented Brede Place, an ancient castle, one wing of which dated from 1378. Much of it was in ruins. It was a gloomy house, with high, vaulted rooms and mysterious towers, filled with strange noises along the dark passageways and through the subterranean passages that had become flooded.

When the Spanish-American War began, Crane returned to the United States to enlist in the navy. He was rejected as physically unfit. Hired as a war correspondent by the New York *World*, he hurried to Cuba, but his luck was bad and he just missed the big story of the Spanish fleet. As he accompanied the army toward the Battle of San Juan Hill, he seemed to the other correspondents to be trying to get himself killed by an indifference to danger that was not so much like bravado as it was like sleepwalking. Yet his war reporting was now first-rate, as it had never been during his experience in Greece.

After nine months, he returned to England. His terrific creative energy held up unabated: before his death at twenty-eight, he wrote forty sketches and tales, five brief novels, three volumes of verse and many journalistic essays—twelve volumes in all. When his expenses and debts had mounted until he needed $1,500 in a month, he was trying desperately to write in spite of his illness. Even when he was taken to the coast in May of 1900, although he was helpless, he was still planning more novels. He died in Germany on June 5, 1900.

Stephen Crane's admirers believe he was potentially one of the world's greatest writers. A biography published in 1950 seriously ranked him with Washington, Jefferson and Lincoln as one of the greatest men in American history. Most of his work does not indicate any exceptional literary quality, however, and some of it makes any claim to greatness seem absurd. He was often hasty and careless, and there are long passages so commonplace that they give no indication of the genius of the author of *The Red Badge of Courage*.

Stephen Crane valued action and adventure for their own sake, but he valued them also because they shocked an audience which had grown accustomed to polite and sentimental fiction. His ideas were violent and defiant for the times in which he lived, but he was not a political reformer, expecting his books to influence men's minds to change the evils he described. He believed that most American writers were affected and unreal, overlooking the harshness of the slums or the derelicts he had known on the Bowery in New York. In his opinion, the genteel writing that was popular was concerned with picturing the life of a handful in the wealthy class. Art for art's sake led to nothing except word-spinning, and American historical fiction was romantic and false, ignoring the anguish and horror of battle. Crane wanted to picture the truth unsparingly, as he saw it, in terms as violent as the life was violent, not for the purpose of starting a crusade, like the socialist writers a little later, but because he believed that an art which glossed over or ignored so much of the American scene could only be narrow at best. "We are most successful in art when we approach nearest to nature and truth," he said.

Much that he did and much that he wrote came from his impulse to shock society out of its complacency—or out of the condition that seemed to young Stephen Crane to be a dull unawareness of the conditions that existed unseen and unmentioned all around the circles of the favored few. He often seemed to have no genuine sympathy for the people whose hardships he pictured. The shocking scenes were rarely as daring as he thought they were. The subject of *Maggie* made publishers reject it, but the tough, lower-class dialect of the story is so exaggerated that it is sometimes almost burlesque, and the book might well have been rejected had it dealt with a different theme.

Crane wasted his genius, says Professor Robert Stallman in an acute essay, and all but threw away his life. He seems never to have realized that his indifference to danger and to opinion made him strange and unusual to many of the people around him. For example, while he was working as a reporter on the New Jersey coast, he purchased a revolver from a cowboy who was raising money to return to the West. Stephen carried the pistol with him when he went to college. He joined a fraternity but did not live in the fraternity house. One night a group of his fraternity brothers, intending to haze him, broke open the door of his room. They found him waiting in the corner, his back to the wall, the revolver in his hand, ready to shoot. He did not understand what they were going to do, and they certainly did not understand him in the slightest. In the same way, he outraged conventions in London or revealed extraordinary coolness under fire at Guantánamo during the Spanish-American War.

And then, too, Stephen Crane's fame was in itself unique. Everyone knew him as the author of a great war book who, at the time he wrote it, had never seen any kind of military action. He was known also as the author, while little more than a boy, of a sympathetic novel about a streetwalker. The result was that Stephen became the target for practical jokes.

Stephen Crane was five feet, six inches tall and weighed 120 pounds. He was thin and not very strong. As his life became a mixture of spurious adventure after he became famous, a real element of danger entered it, for he was not temperamentally fitted to take good-naturedly jokes at his expense. Instead, he challenged every situation to determine what was real and what was artificial in it. A story was circulated that he had become a narcotic addict. He determined to spike the rumor. He made a thorough study of narcotic addiction and wrote a series of articles about it. The articles indicated to people who read them that Stephen Crane knew a great deal about the subject, and so perhaps increased people's suspicions of him.

Yet Stephen won the confidence of discriminating judges to human nature. The great novelist Joseph Conrad took an instant liking to him when he went to England. He said Stephen possessed "a strain of chivalry which made him safe to trust with one's life." The two novelists became close friends. Henry James, whose writing was at the opposite pole from that of Stephen Crane, admired him and, in his last days, befriended him with unfailing generosity. And his one great book, *The Red Badge of Courage*, remains a standing puzzle to all who feel that Crane's admirers have exaggerated his potential contribution. Nothing in the story itself suggests the singular appeal of this strange book. The characters are barely identified. One of the most prominent is known merely as "the tall one." The hero is not even named until near the end of the story. There is a new note in the prose itself, in the interesting, unusual, startling and yet apt descriptive phrases, but aside from the lurid brilliance of the descriptions, the actual content of the book is dullish. A short period of waiting follows each short action, and the actions differ only in intensity. That the hero of the story fights well and then breaks and runs, that he finds his regiment again, returns to action, leads a charge—all this has become familiar as the basic pattern of the book, the change from fear to courage, from youth to manhood.

The strangest quality of *The Red Badge of Courage* is that the battle itself becomes the hero of the story. The battle seems to take on a life of its own, to become independent of the people who are engaged, and the happenings exert an increasingly powerful effect on the imagination because they are a part of it. One reads on to find out what is going to happen to the battle, not what is going to happen to the characters. The characters seem hardly to matter. They are shot, wounded, killed, or they suffer misery, fear and excitement that mounts to exaltation, but their individual fates mean little compared to the fury of the battle itself. Characteristically, Crane speaks of the soldiers seeming "surprised" when they are shot. While it would be too much to say that the wounds in *The Red Badge of Courage* do not seem to hurt, or the deaths in the story to be final, still, it is not too much to say that the image of warfare that emerges from the book is an image of war as it appeared to an incredibly imaginative youth who loved excitement and adventure.

It would be unfair to Stephen Crane, too, to say that he saw the battle as like a game, a sporting event on a gigantic scale. But he loved sport, and *The Red Badge of Courage* expresses the tension of his highly competitive spirit, as it had once been expressed in the games he played. War appeared to him as an intensification of that excitement. The other sides of war, like the illness that kept him from seeing action in Greece or the mismanagement that caused the tragicomedy of gunrunning to Cuba or the hardships and suffering that reach into all parts of life when a society is engaged in war— all this had no meaning to Stephen Crane, for he thought of war as concentrated on the field of battle alone. The cause for which a war is fought seemed not to matter to him. There is only one sentence in *The Red Badge of Courage* touching on the reason why the volunteer is fighting for the Union. That the cause of a war, in the long run, determines the outcome, directs the strategy, inspires the imagination and the heroism, was not a part of Crane's view of war and peace. His life ended before there was a chance to see how his thoughts might have deepened with maturity.

O. Henry
1862-1910

O. Henry

MILLIONS OF HEROES

1862-1910

THE REAL NAME of O. Henry was William Sydney Porter. He was born on September 11, 1862, at Greensboro,
North Carolina. His father was a physician. His mother died
of tuberculosis when he was three years old, his schooling
stopped when he was fifteen, and for five years he worked in
a local drugstore.

At the age of twenty, he went to Texas for his health, as
he was pale and anemic. After two years on a sheep ranch, he
moved to Austin, the capital, in 1884. There he worked in a
real-estate office, sang in a church choir, joined the National
Guard and became a corporal. For four years he was a drafts-
man in the General Land Office. Here were the title deeds,
patents, land grants and legal documents connected with
every foot of land in the state of Texas—a mighty library of
homesteads, honest purchases, cattle ranges, land grabs, railway claims, forgery, theft, perjury and fraud, all on a scale
which young Porter said people who did not know the size
of Texas could not imagine.

Porter married in Austin. His wife bore him two children, one dying in infancy and the other, his daughter Margaret, growing to womanhood. He became a teller there in a

bank and was liked and trusted by the other employees and the president.

In May, 1894, Porter and a friend, with some encouragement from the bank's president, launched a humorous weekly, *The Rolling Stone*. The platform announced: "The politics of The Rolling Stone is Independent with an inclination toward Presbyterianism, and the theory that the world is supported on the back of a mud turtle . . . We believe in personal liberty, but think it is not right to drink forty-seven schooners of beer in a garden on Sunday and then shout *Gotterdammerringheimrihbringzwangingmehrbeerdamkorkzuhellundplazesaherdy* in a strong barreltone voice in the back door of a man who is sincerely trying to figure out Moses' answer to Bob Ingersoll with the aid of a concordance . . ."

Porter was a cartoonist of much ability and filled the pages of *The Rolling Stone* with drawings, jokes, stories and parodies, some of which are very funny. In one of his parodies he tells how he paid a visit to the White House in order to give President Cleveland one of the mementos of *The Rolling Stone*, a round object about the size of a cannonball, with a twist of moss affixed to it. As he held this up before one of the functionaries of the White House: "I saw his hair rise on his head, and he ran like a deer to the door, and, lying down rolled down the long flight of steps into the yard. 'Ah,' said I to myself, 'one of our delinquent subscribers.' Entering the President's office with a beaming smile, he held up the rolling stone. In a husky voice, the President said: 'Wait a moment please.' He fumbled in his pockets until he found a piece of paper with some notes written on it, and rising to his feet, he said in a deep voice, 'I die for Free Trade, my country, and—and—all that sort of thing.' "

The Rolling Stone got off to a good start, with lots of advertising and much Texas support, but the lack of capital and the necessity of making the paper a part-time job after banking hours finally caused its end in the spring of 1895. About the same time a shortage was discovered in Porter's account in the bank. The banking procedures seem to have been very informal and careless, and it is probable that there was no dishonesty on Porter's part. There were stories of shortages amounting to $5,000, but he was eventually charged with a total of $854.08. He had left the bank by this time and was working on the Houston *Post*.

Before his case came to trial, Porter left the United States and settled in Honduras. He knew Spanish and worked as a plantation bookkeeper, a druggist and a printer. Honduras contained many Americans who were under clouds of one kind or another: two Kentuckians, one of whom was guilty of murder; soldiers of fortune; mining promoters; thieves; escaped prisoners; and the famous train robber, Al Jennings, who became Porter's friend.

The illness of his wife led Porter to return to the United States and give himself up. His wife died a few months after his return, and he lived in Austin nearly a year before he was tried. The evidence against him was not strong, but he offered no defense and the fact that he had run away seemed damning proof. He was sentenced to three years and a few months in the Federal penitentiary.

As Leavenworth Penitentiary, the Federal prison, was overcrowded, he served his sentence in Columbus, Ohio. He worked as the prison drug clerk, from five each night until five in the morning. He was number 30664, aged 36, 5'7" tall, with medium chestnut hair sprinkled with gray. The prison physician said he had never known a convict so deeply humiliated by being in prison as Porter. After two years he became secretary to the prison steward, whose office was not in the prison, and was allowed considerable freedom of movement, being permitted to walk about the streets.

Before his trial, he had sold a short story, *The Miracle of Lava Canyon*, to *McClure's Magazine*. In prison he wrote poems and stories of Central America, which he sold to *Ainslee's Magazine*, and a Christmas story, laid in New Orleans, to *McClure's*. These he signed O. Henry. The editors who purchased them did not know that he was a prisoner. By the time he was released, on July 24, 1901, he had sold half a dozen stories, earned $300, and adopted the identity of O. Henry.

O. Henry reached New York in 1902. He found himself merged with the four million inhabitants of the city, a great, miscellaneous teeming center of humanity where he felt free of the sense of disgrace attached to him in places where the individual's past and background are known. He lived in the Hotel Marty on 26th Street between Sixth Avenue and Broadway and there wrote *A Retrieved Reformation*, the story that introduced the famous Jimmy Valentine, an expert safecracker who reforms. But the banker's daughter is locked in the safe, and Jimmy reveals his guilty past in opening the safe vault to free her. Then he expects to be locked up, but the detective says, "Don't believe I recognize you. Your buggy's waitin' for you, aint it?"

O. Henry sold *A Retrieved Reformation* for $250 and the dramatic rights for $500. He was asked to write a play on the subject himself, but turned it down. The play, called *Alias Jimmy Valentine*, became one of the most famous popular successes in American theatrical history and the playwright earned $100,000.

O. Henry spent his time talking to the loungers in Madison Park near his hotel, getting to know policemen, store clerks, waitresses, salesmen, pickpockets, gangsters, broken-down prize fighters and ex-circus performers. He haunted vaudeville houses, roof gardens, the Bowery, the theatrical district and the small restaurants off 14th Street, where he was a favored patron because of his friendliness and his generous tips. Sometimes he walked all night up the streets from the Lower East Side to the bright lights of Broadway. Sometimes he spent days at Coney Island. He dressed quietly, was courteous and polite, said little, and looked around when he entered a restaurant before sitting down, as if fearing to see someone he knew.

O. Henry hated to write. There was no question of selling his stories: he could sell them long in advance. Nor was there any question of something to write about: he was always surprised at the city, at the astonishing careers of the citizens who peopled it, at something always happening around the corner. A group of newspapermen at dinner with O. Henry asked him where he found his plots. "Everywhere," O. Henry said. "There are stories in everything." He picked up the menu. "There's a story in this," he commented. To prove it he wrote *Springtime à la Carte*. In O. Henry's background were the cowboys and rustlers and gunmen he had known when he first entered Texas, the outlaws and adventurers in Central America, the underworld figures he had met in prison, and now around him, in the teeming city whose magic always absorbed him, there were four million mysterious strangers to whom almost anything might happen between sunrise and sunset.

The problem lay in compressing the material into the neat, precise, economical form he had invented. O. Henry's stories are usually only five pages long. The famous *The Gift of the Magi* is told in four pages, or 2,015 words. Very few of these words are wasted. The situation in the story is complex and unusual. A young wife whose great beauty lies in her wonderful hair has nothing to give her husband as a Christmas present. The young husband has no possessions of value except a fine watch. The wife cuts off her hair, sells it for $20, and buys a watch chain as her husband's present. She busies herself trying to make her bobbed hair look attractive, fearing her husband will think she is no longer beautiful, but when he comes home he stares at her with an expression she cannot fathom, a kind of wonder and stupefaction: he has sold his wonderful watch to buy her two beautiful combs. "Here," said O. Henry, "I have lamely related to you the uneventful chronicle of two foolish children in a flat who most unwisely sacrificed for each other the greatest treasures of their house . . . Of all who give gifts, these two were the wisest."

O. Henry's stories generally began with some individual in a perplexing situation. A prominent man about town discovers that his quiet and retiring wife is stunningly beautiful and a terrific social success. A bum learns that he is to be restored to his family fortune the next day and lives in terror lest something happen to him before morning—a tree might fall on him or a stone drop from a building or he might go blind or have a heart attack before he has a chance to enjoy his fortune. A quiet and inconspicuous family man walks around the corner to buy a cigar, gets into a fight, and battles with such outraged ferocity that he is taken for a great fighter and hired to be the bodyguard of an heiress. In each story the last paragraph, almost the last sentence, wraps up the whole complex plot in a solution that is generally amusing, sometimes touching, sometimes hilarious burlesque, as in *The Ransom of Red Chief*, in which the kidnapers who have stolen a mean Southern boy finally pay his father to take him back. Many of these effects are mechanical, a matter of trickery and artifice, but often the setting, the characters, the plot and the sudden solution are fused by a warmth of feeling and a spontaneous humor into works of art.

O. Henry wrote fifty-one of these stories in 1903 and sixty-six in 1904. The range of setting and the variety of characters prevented them from becoming monotonous: he wrote of all-night restaurants, furnished rooms, brownstone houses "that looked like a recently excavated bowling alley in Pompeii," Central Park, police stations, fashionable clubs, glittering hotels, corner saloons. To vary the background, he wrote of the Diamond Cross Ranch in a little valley of the Candad Verda in the wonderful story of *The Marquis and Miss Sally;* of a Latin American port, a Texas killer and a crooked American consul in the masterly *A Double-Dyed Deceiver.*

In collaboration with the reformed train robber, Al Jennings, he wrote *Holding Up a Train*, an exact description of the method, timing and plan of the operation. His letter to Jennings on what the account should contain is a model of journalistic instruction that throws a good deal of light on his own way of working. "Give it *life* and the vitality of *facts*," he wrote to the old robber. "Describe the *facts* and *details* . . . Begin abruptly, without any philosophizing, with your ideas of the best times, places and conditions for a hold-up—compare your opinions of this with those of others—mention some poorly conceived attempts and failures of others, giving your opinion why—as far as possible refer to actual occurrences and incidents—describe the manner of a hold-up, how many men is best, where they are generally stationed, how do they generally go into it, nervous? or joking? or solemnly?"

With his astonishing fertility of invention and his ceaseless interest in all kinds of details, O. Henry avoided monotony also by the tone of his writing. His style was bright and neat, his comments surrounding the story with an agreeable patter as the plot unfolded, like a stage magician distracting the audience until, with a sudden flourish, he reveals the rabbit in the hat, the right card drawn from the deck or some other astonishing feat of sleight of hand. In the same way, O. Henry suddenly revealed the surprise finish of his tales.

The New York *World* gave him a contract to write one story each week for its Sunday edition. O. Henry dreaded settling down to work, and would put it off as long as possible. The *World* assigned a copy boy to stay with O. Henry and follow him around, rushing his copy to the office as soon as he wrote anything. O. Henry quickly made friends with the copy boy, told him his troubles, appealed to his sympathies, and soon had the copy boy on his side in his ceaseless attempt to evade the editors. Through the last part of the week, O. Henry and the copy boy lingered over long dinners in expensive restaurants. With the deadline actually upon him, O. Henry would start to write. When he finished a page, the copy boy rushed it to the *World* office on Park Row, where the printers were waiting to set it up. At the last minute, just before the presses had to roll, or the Sunday newspapers would be late, O. Henry furnished the last lines, the inevitable surprise finish of the story.

Few of his friends knew of his trouble with the bank that had led to his arrest and imprisonment. Much of the money that he earned went to provide a good education and care for his daughter Margaret. The strain of making each story come out right every week took a heavy toll of his nervous energy, and he tried to reform by writing early in the week, before the deadline. Once he even wrote a number of stories in a few days, to give himself several weeks rest. But then, as he needed money, he sold these stories to another magazine and faced the same last-minute crisis again.

He had become the most widely read storyteller in the United States. His first book, *Cabbages and Kings* (1904), contained his Central American stories, and the second, *The Four Million*, his first tales of New York. Others followed swiftly: *The Trimmed Lamp* in 1907 and *Heart of the West* in the same year, *The Voice of the City* in 1908, *Road of Destiny* and *Options* in 1909, *Strictly Business* and *Whirligigs* in 1910. Three more collections were brought out after his death. In all, 236 stories are included in his collected works.

O. Henry married again, in 1907, this time the daughter of a prominent family from his native state of North Carolina. In his last years his fame made it easy for him to collect in advance on stories he planned to write, so that he soon owed stories to many publications. His expenses increased, as he lived well, and he was constantly badgered by editors for material he had promised them. Sometimes he collected from one magazine for a story but then sold it to another and wrote something else for the first. He was writing a typical O. Henry story when he died on June 5, 1910, at the age of forty-seven.

The pressure under which he worked and the confining limits of his form narrowed his work beyond his true ability. O. Henry was an entertainer and an almost unfailing one, like a top-notch vaudeville performer who never let his audience down. He made no claim to being a serious artist. The picture of American life that he gradually built up is an almost accidental creation, and yet it is one of immense variety and in-

terest, composed of thousands of terse scenes, each distinct
and different, street-corner meetings and extraordinary coincidences all contributing to an impression of patternless movement and restless drifting, as if the whole population were
always in motion. A man from New England could expect to
meet his neighbor in the Arizona desert or in the ballroom of
the Waldorf Astoria as naturally as on the streets of his home
town.

There were coincidences in many of O. Henry's stories,
wildly improbable, as he cheerfully acknowledged. In fact,
his stories depended on coincidence. But were they really so
extraordinary? If a man who lived in a village met his neighbor at the bank, it did not seem strange or unusual. The America that O. Henry pictured was an enormous village, a continental small town, with millions of heroes of stories jostling
each other all the time, where the people were pretty much
alike, and the old familiar patterns of village culture persisted
in the midst of millions of people and over thousands of miles
of country. Americans lived on a grand scale, or, like O.
Henry himself, they circulated among strangers, but they
were still essentially villagers, and at each crisis in their lives
something like a guardian angel (or a destroying nemesis)
stepped in and changed the outcome. O. Henry's America
was a land of strange coincidences. The result of the coincidence, whether it was an accidental encounter or a stroke of
luck, was generally beneficent—somebody benefited or a
good deed was rewarded or poetic justice was done. That was
the side of American life that interested O. Henry, and he
saw stories of that nature in inexhaustible abundance all
around him.

Jack London
1876-1916

Jack London

MELODRAMA

 1876-1916

Jack London's *The Call of the Wild* began with the theft of a dog from a ranch in the Santa Clara Valley of California. The discovery of gold in the Klondike had made any dog capable of becoming a sled dog worth its weight in gold. And Buck, half Saint Bernard and half Scotch shepherd, weighing 140 pounds, was plainly in line to become the leader of a dog team if he could be moved to Alaska.

In four days of writing, Jack London hurried Buck's story through the episodes in which the dog was stolen, through the train ride that bewildered him, through a big scene of a savage beating at the hands of a dog trainer. Well cared for all his life, accustomed only to kindness at the hands of mankind, Buck learned fast. He survived the voyage on the *Narwhal* to Seattle and on the beach learned something new about dogs—the loser in a Northern dog fight was killed by dogs who gathered around to watch the outcome of the battle. Then there followed the scenes of Buck's training as one of nine huskies pulling a dog sled—a succession of harsh experiences that broke the dog without breaking his spirit.

The scene that made the dog a living creature came early in the book. Terrified by the snow, shivering and miserable,

Buck tried to find a place to sleep. The other dogs seemed to have disappeared. Buck wandered hopelessly in the darkness until suddenly the snow caved in beneath him. The dogs were sleeping warm and snug beneath the snow, completely buried, protected against the wind and storm overhead. Buck dug a cavern in the snow near them, was soon covered over, and "in a trice the heat from his body filled the confined space and he was asleep."

Jack London wrote the first four thousand words of his most famous story in four days. He knew he had a best seller. The time was 1903, and Jack London was a twenty-seven-year-old writer who was just beginning to be known. He intended to make *The Call of the Wild* a short story, but as he saw its possibilities he put everything else aside and let the story of Buck in the Far North take him wherever it would— scenes of the dogs tangled in the harness; scenes of hauling the sled past snowdrifts hundreds of feet deep, over the great Chilcoot Divide into "the sad and lonely North"; scenes of the dogs starving on the trail; of rescues, battles, escapes; of terrible overwork hauling freight, and of racing drives hauling the mail; scenes in which dogs who were like Buck, once domesticated, felt their kinship with the wolves and howled in the night, "with the aurora borealis flaming coldly overhead, or the stars leaping in the frost dance, and the land numb and frozen under its pall of snow."

Jack London sent *The Call of the Wild* to *The Saturday Evening Post*. The answer came back at once: a check for $2,000. He had written the story in exactly thirty days. The publishing house of Macmillan, which had begun to publish his books, paid him another $2,000 outright to publish it in book form. The publishers suggested that Jack London sell them all rights to *The Call of the Wild*, instead of a contract on the usual royalty basis, and they would put the extra money into advertising. London agreed. If he had taken royalties, he would have earned $100,000 from *The Call of the Wild*. But he did not regret his bargain for, although he received only the $2,000, his name became so famous that his writing was soon earning him $75,000 a year.

Jack London was born in San Francisco on January 12, 1876. His parents were a wandering couple who gave spiritualistic séances and lectures on phrenology. Before his birth they separated, and his mother became the subject of a tragic newspaper story when she attempted to commit suicide. After Jack was born, she married John London, who had been a soldier in the Union army and a sheriff in the frontier country of Idaho. John London was devoted to his foster son. Through the years of boyhood, while John London ran a grocery store in Oakland, California, or set up a series of farms in California, Jack was at the side of the quiet, reserved man, hunted and fished with him, and regarded himself as his son.

While they were living on an eighty-acre farm near Livermore, California, Jack ran across a book that made a profound impression on him: Washington Irving's *Alhambra*. He developed a taste for reading which was combined with his love of outdoor life. When the family returned to Oakland he haunted the public library. The librarian became interested in him and guided him to authors he liked: Melville, Kipling, Stevenson and the old English novelist Smollett.

It was fortunate that Jack developed his habit of reading when he did, for shortly after, a series of misfortunes wrecked the family finances and he had little time for books. Jack delivered papers, worked on an ice wagon, set pins in a bowling alley, and every cent of the $12 he earned each month was needed by the family for food.

At fifteen, with money borrowed from a nurse who had worked for the Londons in a more prosperous period, he bought a boat and began raiding the privately owned oyster beds that lined the bay. Before dawn he raced the oysters to restaurants and markets and for a time made money fast. He had fights with boys and men in the same racket, and was nearly killed when his boat was burned. But before he landed in jail, as most of the oyster pirates eventually did, he received an unexpected offer to join the state Fish Patrol. This gave him the excitement and the outdoor life that he liked and also kept him safely out of harm's way.

At sixteen, Jack London sailed on the schooner *Sophia Sutherland* to Japan and the coast of Siberia, hunting seals. Later, a trip across the United States as a hobo (during which he kept a meticulous account of his experiences) convinced him that he needed an education. At nineteen, he enrolled as a freshman in Oakland High School.

After two years he left, crammed for five weeks, and passed the entrance examinations of the University of California. His grades were good, but family finances soon forced him to give up college and return to work.

Gold was discovered on Bonanza Creek in an almost inaccessible area of the Klondike in 1896. A wild rush started for the Far North. On March 12, 1897, Jack London joined some thirty thousand other gold seekers who poured into Alaska on their way to the gold fields. He found no gold, but during a winter at the mouth of the Steward River, from the stories of passing prospectors who sought shelter in his cabin, he found a rich mine of material that supplied him with stories all his life.

Of these stories of the North, *The Call of the Wild* was

his best. The animal that is tamed, and yet dimly remembers the wild state, driven into the wilderness by the savagery of men, won back to civilization by the kindliness of a good master, running with a wolf pack after his master is killed, summed up Jack London's view of nature and formed a fitting symbol of his philosophy.

By the time *The Call of the Wild* had made him world-famous, Jack London was already well known around San Francisco and Oakland. While still in high school he became a socialist, made speeches on street corners, and was written up in the newspapers as The Boy Socialist. He also wrote stories for local magazines, including the high-school magazine, and by the time he was twenty-three had stories and articles appearing in five different national magazines in a single month. After his return from Alaska, he sold Gold Rush stories to *McClures, Youth's Companion, The Atlantic Monthly* and others, and was written up in the newspapers as The Boy Author.

Soon after he married in 1900, Jack London ran for mayor of Oakland on the socialist ticket and received 245 votes. He was hired as a correspondent to cover the Boer War, but when he got to London, his assignment was abruptly dropped. He dressed in old clothes and lived in the East End, the slums of London, gathering material for a book: *The People of the Abyss.*

Back in America, with the first $2,000 that he earned from *The Call of the Wild,* Jack bought a boat, the *Spray.* He wrote each morning, usually beginning about five o'clock, put in eight hours, finishing one thousand words a day, then sailed his boat or fished and shot ducks in the marsh until dark. When domestic conflicts interrupted his work on his next novel, *The Sea Wolf,* he anchored the *Spray* at the mouth of the Sacramento River and remained aboard until he had completed the book. *The Sea Wolf* is an intense melodrama, climaxing in the conflict of a savage and partly irrational sea captain, who stands for primitive man, a human comparable to the return to the savage state of Buck in *The Call of the Wild*. Opposed to him is a normal man who represents civilization, pitted against an amoral brute who mastered civilization's techniques. *The Sea Wolf* was an instantaneous success. Forty thousand orders for the book were received before it was published.

During the Russo-Japanese War, Jack London served as a war correspondent. The reporters were kept in Tokyo and not permitted to visit the front. Jack London chartered a native junk and sailed to Korea, nearly perishing of hardships on the way. He got as far as the Yalu River before the Japanese authorities arrested and imprisoned him. While he was in Seoul in prison, it was reported that he was to be executed, and a wave of protests mounted.

He was released and returned to the United States to a bigger popular following than ever. At this point, two ruinous projects formed in Jack London's adventurous mind. One project was to sail around the world. The other was to build a great house, a perfect home for a successful writer. He had purchased a ranch in the beautiful Valley of the Moon in California, paying only $7,000 for 130 acres of redwoods, live oaks, madroña and manzanita—a great bargain, for the region had not become known as ideal vacation land. But his dream castle was a nightmare, planned with the utmost care, with no expense to be spared in selecting the right material and getting the best craftsmen to work the stone and the wood, but left unsupervised in the building. Jack London was often away, and fantastic sums were charged to him for work that was not done. The supposedly fine walls were really hollow. Before the house was finished, Jack London began another large-scale improvement in a ranch, spending money so recklessly that a single foolhardy experiment in planting eucalyptus trees cost him $46,862 and brought in no return.

Jack London had become so successful an author that he might have succeeded in building Wolf House and might even have successfully developed his model ranch. But only a millionaire with unlimited credit could have also undertaken at the same time to build a boat in which to sail around the world. Jack began the *Snark* at a time when his expenses on his house were already enormous. He hired a friend to do the actual construction and gave him a free hand. He was still unworried about his mounting bills, for he expected to be able to sell articles to magazines as the *Snark* sailed to the South Sea Islands and into the Far East. The *Snark* was a forty-five-foot craft, and Jack expected to spend seven years in circumnavigating the globe. Since he got $750 or more for an article, the financial problem did not seem an impossible one.

The *Snark* was so long in building, however, that Jack London's world cruise became a joke. In desperation, he decided to sail to Honolulu and put the finishing touches on the boat there. Jack London's first marriage had ended in a divorce, and his second wife, Charmian, accompanied him on many of his adventures. She planned to sail around the world, too, and also write books on the voyage.

The *Snark* was crushed between two barges as the cruise to Honolulu began. Moved toward the ways, she stuck stern first in the mud. Twice a day for a week, at every high tide, two tugs tried to pull her free. When the windlass on the *Snark* was employed to help, the casting broke, the gears ground, and the windlass was ruined. When Jack turned on the seventy-horsepower motor, the bedplate reared up in the air, smashing all connections, and fell on its side.

Everyone he knew seemed to be laughing about his misadventure. But it was no joke to him. His expenses had mounted to the incredible sum of $30,000 a month. Jack London maintained expensive homes for his first wife and daughters and another home for his mother, who had quarreled with Charmian London. More than $80,000 was spent on Wolf House, and it was still not complete. In addition, Jack London spent about $35,000 a year on hospitality. A small army of friends and acquaintances, picturesque characters he had met, ex-convicts, strangers who appeared from nowhere, lived on his bounty. All told, Jack London earned a million dollars by his writing, but while his income was $75,000 a year, his expenses were $100,000 a year.

The *Snark* eventually put to sea with Jack and Charmian aboard, and a crew of four men. None of these knew anything of navigation, and only one, the future explorer Martin Johnson, was even a good sailor. Jack and his wife and Johnson did most of the actual sailing, under increasingly hazardous conditions, as the *Snark*, badly built despite the $35,000 invested in her, reached the South Seas. There Jack's hands began to swell as a result of ultraviolet rays during long exposure to the sun. The mysterious illness affected his whole body, and he was rushed to a hospital in Australia. After two years, the trip around the world was abandoned, and the *Snark* sold at auction for $3,000.

Meanwhile, the building of Wolf House had gone on with even greater waste in his absence. Expenses not even remotely connected with his affairs were charged to him, and he was soon bankrupt. However, a novel he had written on shipboard before his illness, *Martin Eden*, his own story, thinly disguised, was another success and saved him from financial ruin. In a single year after his return, by intense labor, with stories and articles appearing almost constantly, Jack London rebuilt his fortune. By the spring of 1913 he was the highest-paid, best-known and most popular author in the world.

While he lived at the Valley of the Moon, preparing to move into his dream house, Jack London enjoyed a return to his old hospitable days. There were generally ten or twenty guests around his place—socialist comrades, old friends, friends of friends—who came and left in the haze of his miscellaneous benevolence. He was still an active socialist, constantly lecturing and writing for the cause. He generally needed only five hours sleep. He still rose at five, wrote a thousand words on the story or novel at hand, then answered letters, sometimes dictating a hundred a day. By one o'clock, after working eight hours, he joined the assembled guests who were waiting for him. Before he appeared, a dead silence was demanded. After lunch, saddle horses were brought, and the whole party rode under the redwoods or swam in the pool London had built or watched the slow building of Wolf House. At night, Jack London read until late, going over books and magazines for material he wanted, studying government reports, making notes for future writing.

At two o'clock on the morning of August 18, 1913, the day before Jack London was to move into his new home, Wolf House burned to the ground. There were reports that a former friend had set fire to it, that an ex-convict had been responsible, that some of the people involved in the building had burned it down, but nothing was proved.

Jack London had not lost heart under terrific adversity,

but the destruction of his house almost crushed him. He tried to go on writing, but the elasticity seemed to have gone out of his temperament and the vitality to have left his work. By the time he was forty years old, he had written fifty books. Several of the later ones—*Burning Daylight, John Barleycorn, The Valley of the Moon, The Star Rover, Before Adam* and *White Fang* (the sequel to *The Call of the Wild*)—had the quality and some of the popularity of his best books, despite the extreme pressure under which they were written. He was found dead of morphine poisoning on November 22, 1916.

His fame rests most solidly on *The Call of the Wild*. In that story the innate kindliness that led to the socialist campaigns of his youth and made him an easy mark for anyone who appealed to his sympathy in his days of wealth found a creative outlet. A civilized animal pitted against the wilderness was the theme of much that he wrote, and he wrote best when his central character was a dog who enlisted the reader's sympathy rather than a complex human being whose reactions were never so simple.

Modern American
Writers

Modern American Writers

WILLIAM DEAN HOWELLS - HAMLIN GARLAND - THEODORE
DREISER - JOHN DOS PASSOS - ERSKINE CALDWELL - JAMES
FARRELL - WILLIAM FAULKNER - ERNEST HEMINGWAY -
VAN WYCK BROOKS

IN THE EARLY days of American literature, the major
American writers were constantly struggling to record the
life of their native land without coming under the dominance
of literary styles or habits of thought that had been formed in
the Old World.

Each writer, in his own way, wanted to give expression
to the new and exciting life around him, and to the promise
of a new kind of society that was found in American democracy. But they had grown up with their imaginations
shaped by their reading of the authors of Europe. Inevitably,
they were forced to interpret the New World in terms that
were drawn from the Old. So James Fenimore Cooper followed Sir Walter Scott even while he opposed him. Cooper
wrote his first sea story, *The Pilot,* because he realized after
reading one of Scott's tales of pirates that Scott knew nothing
of the sea. And Mark Twain wrote many of his books in the

spirit of *A Connecticut Yankee at King Arthur's Court* to ridicule Old World notions of an ideal human society.

With the Declaration of Independence and the Constitution, the founders of the republic created a new kind of government in the history of the world. They denied that human society must be governed by one man or by one class. They denied that mankind was inherently divided into inferior and superior classes, with each man's place forever determined by his birth. They affirmed that all men were equal under God, that each had a right to life, liberty and the pursuit of happiness. They declared that just government rested upon the consent of the governed and that the objective of government was to promote the common welfare, to provide for the common defense, and to insure domestic tranquillity.

These were assertions of magnificent faith and tremendous power; they are so now. But there was a formidable task laid upon the imaginative writers of the United States who tried to translate them into stories laid against the background of ordinary American life. They had read the stories and poems written by gifted men over the long centuries—men who had always lived under monarchies, who took it as a matter of course that society should be divided into classes, with class war between them, and who believed, with Old World wisdom, that there would be little change in the future. The vision of our early writers was refracted as it passed through the lens of learning created in an older culture.

They did not want to cut themselves off from the world's inheritance of literature. They wanted to extend the benefits of civilization, of learning, of art, of science, of material prosperity, to all men. To create a literature which would rank with the finest of the older societies, to surround the native places of home with significant associations, to show the world that there would be no lowering of standards in a society where the governed determined their own fate—these were motives that sustained writers through lifetimes of solitary labor, produced a magnificent literary heritage, and gave to American literature a distinctive, original and poignant quality which has never left it.

Our early writers were inspired also by the desire to record, or to build an imaginative fabric upon, the life of the unspoiled continent that lay around them. When James Fenimore Cooper published his first novel, there were perhaps four million white people in America, some seven hundred thousand Negro slaves and an unknown number of Indians, perhaps three or four million. West of the thirteen states lay a continental wilderness too vast for the imagination to grasp. Beyond a thousand miles of wilderness there stretched a thousand miles of prairie, and beyond this immense waste were the Rockies, mysterious, nameless mountains that were then believed to be the haunt of prehistoric animals. The wild life of the continent was beyond calculation. The best scientific estimate is that there were then four hundred million to five hundred million beaver, sixty million buffalo, fifty-three million deer, forty million antelope, ten million wolves, five hundred thousand bears and billions of gray squirrels and small animals. The wild bird population was in proportion. There were millions of wild geese, ducks, turkeys, grouse and passenger pigeons. This last bird, now extinct, was large and brightly plumaged. It was once so numerous that Alexander Wilson, the first American ornithologist, saw a single flock 240 miles long, numbering 2,230,000,000, and James Audubon a few years later calculated that only one of the many continuous streams that he saw during the migrating season contained at least 1,100,000,000 birds.

When the early American writers criticized American life, they were not criticizing democracy, but the aspects of American life that fell short of the promise of the New World. Cooper described the senseless slaughter of passenger pigeons and the despoiling of nature; Hawthorne the smuggling of merchants; Melville the brutality of floggings on shipboard; Mark Twain the callousness of frontier towns. They did not mean that democracy had failed because these evils existed. Their criticism was doubly powerful because they sincerely felt *such things should not be in America*. Every other country on earth and every society of the past contained features as bad or worse. But there was a profoundly patriotic motive in the criticisms of our early writers, for they attacked ancient evils, not as inherent in man's nature and society, but as something foreign to the spirit of the nation.

When the United States was weak in a material sense, its appeal to the imagination and sympathy of mankind everywhere was strong. As the United States grew strong in a material sense, a new note of doubt and questioning came into the expressions of its imaginative life that made up its literature. What was the source of this doubt? The magnificent work of the early writers had freed Americans of their awe of the Old World masters. The tremendous material growth of the United States had shown the world that democracy could outstrip the world in the production of material goods. Some of the doubt arose because with the increasing strength of the United States and the industrial expansion of the country another form of inequality came into being. Yet in the early days of the United States our writers had not lost heart even though there existed in the South an institution—Negro slavery—that contradicted the very purpose of the new nation and made its claim to equality ridiculous to Old World critics.

The new note that came into American writing as the United States grew strong was described by Emerson. "A new disease has fallen on the life of man," he said. "Every Age, like every human body, has its own distemper. Other times have had war, or famine, or a barbarism domestic or bordering, as their antagonism. Our forefathers walked in the world and went to their graves, tormented with the fear or Sin, and the terror of the Day of Judgement. These terrors have lost their force, and our torment is Unbelief, the Uncertainty as to what we ought to do; the distrust of the value of what we do, and the distrust that the Necessity (which we all at last believe in) is fair and beneficient." When our writers looked around them, they saw on all sides conditions that were foreign to the promise of democracy—slums as ominous and as dangerous as the forest had ever been; the waste of natural resources on a scale that made the luxury of the kings seem petty; inequalities for the Negroes that made a mockery of their freedom; political corruption that weakened the very claim of the United States to be based upon the consent of the governed. The forest had been cleared, as Francis Parkman had said, and the nation had grown strong, but there was much within it that did not seem a part of that cause for which the Founding Fathers had risked their lives, their fortune and their sacred honor. The Unbelief of which Emerson wrote settled deeply into the work of American writers and threatened to become chronic.

To the socialist writers, like Jack London, or to the communist writers later on, the solution was simple. Democracy had failed; there was an inevitable conflict between the ruling class and the ruled, which could only be ended by revolution.

But to most American writers, human reality was more complex. They did not believe the proposed remedy would change anything, for there would still remain the conflict of the governing class and the governed, even though the governing class might call itself communist or socialist—a continuation in another form of the conflict the United States had been formed to end. The whole concept of an inevitable class war had come into being in Europe, in the midst of Old World habits of thought; it was foreign to the spirit of American literature. If they accepted it, American writers were compelled to reject the inheritance of their great predecessors, both the political masters, unparalleled in world history, who had framed the American constitution, and the writers who had clothed American life in images of enduring significance.

Novelists like William Dean Howells and Hamlin Garland, who wrote in the period after the Civil War, saw clearly the inequalities that were hardening into fixed patterns in American life, but they did not, for that reason, reject the basis of American democracy. Howells (1837–1920) was a printer, born in Ohio, who became a newspaper writer while still in his teens. He wrote a campaign biography of Abraham Lincoln, spent four years as consul in Venice, and became editor of *The Atlantic Monthly* in 1872. Howells was a realist, trying to picture life "with entire fidelity in all its commonplaceness," and his best books, *The Rise of Silas Lapham* and *A Hazard of New Fortunes*, were unsparing accounts of familiar American characters and scenes. Hamlin Garland (1860–1940) was a farm boy, born in Wisconsin, who made his way to Boston, educated himself in the public library, taught, lectured, and wrote moving accounts of prairie life in *Main Traveled Roads* (1891) and *A Little Norske* (1893).

These men tried to retain balance and perspective in their criticism of American life, but their work lacked excitement and drama. Indeed, it is only the lucid charm of Howell's style that makes him readable, and a poignant quality, a suppressed poetic fervor, that lifts Hamlin Garland's work above a drab portrayal of the commonplace.

The next great realistic novelist, Theodore Dreiser (1871–1945), went far byond them in his relentless portrayal of American poverty, and in the flat, literal, opaque style in which he wrote. The son of a pious German immigrant, born in Terre Haute, Indiana, Dreiser became a newspaperman and then the successful and enterprising editor of a woman's magazine. His first and best book, *Sister Carrie*, was published in 1900 but was scarcely read until twenty years later, when Dreiser's writing suddenly became popular. In his years of obscurity, he brought out *Jennie Gerhardt* (1911) and a series of novels, including *The Financier* (1912) and *The Titan* (1914), showing the ruthless rise to power of a great capital-ist. Dreiser's writing was almost formless, a plodding recital enlivened only by the clarity of his familiar American scenes, yet often moving in its simplicity and in the fumbling honesty with which he approached problems his contemporaries ignored. The satires of Sinclair Lewis (1885–1951), especially *Main Street* (1920) and *Babbit* (1922), pictured American provincial culture and American businessmen in the grip of a passion for conformity so relentless as to be paralyzing to any form of human independence whatsoever.

John Dos Passos tried to get away from the flat literalness that weakened Dreiser's novels. He incorporated into his 1,500-page trilogy, *U.S.A.*, a series of brilliant thumbnail sketches of famous Americans, from Henry Ford to popular movie stars, whose real lives were indirectly reflected in the happenings in the novel. Another of the interludes in the novel contained autobiographical impressions suggesting the point of view from which Dos Passos had witnessed the times of which he wrote. Born in Chicago in 1896, the son of a corporation lawyer, Dos Passos graduated from Harvard, served in the first World War, and wrote one of the first novels based upon it, *Three Soldiers*. More than any other novelist of his generation, Dos Passos tried to encompass in *U.S.A.* the whole life of the United States in all its complexity and growth. There is a tremendous range of setting and character in the long book, and in many places it seems really to unmask American society. But there is also a curious narrowness in the action, the same kind of characters appearing in each section of the country and in every walk of life, and the deliberate diffuseness of the book and the haphazardness that pervades it, suggest how difficult a task the novelist faces in translating contemporary America into fiction.

There is rarely in Dreiser's novels, or in the fiction of the writers who followed him, a sense that the author has written because he is deeply interested in the character. Writers did not write in the spirit of Mark Twain sketching in Huckleberry Finn, because the experiences were funny. They wrote to prove a case. It is impossible to feel that Dreiser had the slightest sympathy for the hero of his long series of novels about a financier: he was simply analyzing a man of wealth because he considered him to be representative of the real rulers of the country and responsible for its inequalities. The powerful early novels of Erskine Caldwell and James Farrell were not written because their authors came upon subjects that fascinated them but because the subjects confirmed their beliefs. Caldwell, the son of a Georgia clergyman, was born in 1903, became a newspaperman after working at a wide variety of jobs throughout the South, and in *Tobacco Road* (1932) and *God's Little Acre* (1933) produced two of the most appalling records of rural poverty ever penned. Farrell, born in Chicago in 1904, wrote *Studs Lonigan* (1932), portraying with unsparing honesty and a controlled absence of sympathy the wrecking of a boy who becomes a hoodlum through the casual, purposeless, machinelike operation of the society in which he lives. Both authors wrote many other novels, but only their first works equaled Dreiser's realism and his indictment of American life.

The picture of America that emerges from the novels of Ernest Hemingway and William Faulkner is a harsh one, but the writing of both authors contains redeeming elements of interest in the scene itself—hunting and fishing in the woods in Hemingway's stories, and a ceaseless absorption in the picturesque characters, folkways and interrelations of his native Mississippi in Faulkner's work. William Faulkner was born in New Albany, Mississippi, in 1897, and grew up in near-by Oxford, the site of the state university. His family was long established in the region, his great-grandfather, a colonel in the Confederate army, having been a railroad builder, a plantation owner and the author of a sensationally popular novel in the eighties.

William Faulkner served in the Canadian Air Force in the first World War. Returning to Mississippi, he wrote *Soldier's Pay* and *Mosquitoes*, sardonic studies of modern American life, and *Sartoris*, based in part on the story of his own family. Faulkner began writing, like Melville, in a flippant and casual spirit. He was halfway through *Sartoris* when he "discovered," he said, "that writing was a mighty fine thing." He had learned that the process of creating a fictional character true to the life of his time added dignity to men, and without knowing it, he came to a purpose like Hawthorne's: to seek out the true and indestructible values that were hidden under the surface of life.

In a terrific burst of creative energy, Faulkner wrote the four novels that made him a major figure in American fiction: *The Sound and the Fury* and *Sanctuary*, both written in 1929, as was *Sartoris* also; *As I Lay Dying* (1930); *Light in August* (1932). In *As I Lay Dying* and *Light in August*, Faulkner revealed a mastery of backwoods dialect and habits of thought unequaled by any other American writer. *Sanctuary* was intended by Faulkner to be a thriller, a hack job, sensational and violent, but the story itself is so tense and sustained that it rises above its limitations. *The Sound and the Fury* is a difficult, entangled story, almost a cipher in its complexity, a tale of the decay of a Southern family, but with its brilliant illumination brought into so sharp a focus that it remains as powerful as any novel in American literature.

Faulkner's other novels range from stories of flying, like *Pylon* (1935), to war stories, notably *A Fable* (1954). Much of his work is dense and confused, but the focus of his books is generally sharp when concentrated on his native region. His best novels and stories are laid in the mythical town of Jefferson. The same characters and families and settings appear again and again, and Faulkner has gradually built up an entire community in deep perspective and reality. In this community there has been in the past a simpler and more harmonious life, something like what Mark Twain pictured in Hannibal, but existing under a patrician plantation order of aloof responsibility. Gradually a new spirit has taken over the town, symbolized by the monstrous Snopes family. These are people who are essentially amoral, making their way by any and all means, infiltrating the life of the whole area, grafting, wheedling, ceaselessly plotting and planning, climbing always, and fighting so unscrupulously that the more civilized inhabitants are restrained by their own higher standards from opposing them effectively.

Ernest Hemingway was born in Oak Park, Illinois, near Chicago, in 1898. His father was a physician. Hemingway attended Oak Park High School, played football, contributed stories to the high-school paper, and after being graduated worked on a newspaper in Kansas City. During the first World War, Hemingway served in Italy, and was badly wounded. Becoming a newspaperman in Toronto, and later a Paris correspondent for Canadian newspapers, he began to write extremely condensed little stories, sometimes only a paragraph, that were generally only isolated glimpses of war —a wounded man trying to joke; an execution in the rain. These Hemingway followed with stories of fishing in the Michigan woods that awakened interest because of the extraordinary freshness and clarity of his prose. No American writer equaled his ability to get at the savor of outdoor experience—fresh air and solitude, running streams, and trees and river banks—visualized so powerfully that the very prose seemed to have inhaled the fresh oxygen of the scene. There are comparable passages in Parkman and Melville and Thoreau, but they are almost incidental to the author's purposes, surrounded by comment and speculation, an observation of a moment. For Hemingway, the experience itself—a fishing trip, as in *Big Two-Hearted River;* a meal in the woods; a storm—was its own justification.

Hemingway's first popular book was *The Sun Also Rises,* dealing with American expatriates in Europe, published in 1926. A war novel based on his experiences in Italy, *A Fare-*

well to Arms, was brought out in 1929, followed by a novel about a hard-bitten Florida rumrunner, *To Have and to Have Not* (1937), and a novel on the Civil War in Spain, *For Whom the Bell Tolls* (1940). A terrific impact, almost a revolution in popular taste, had been worked by Hemingway's terse style, especially by the stories that were collected in *In Our Time* and *Men Without Women.* A generation of imitators set to work, turning out stories of violent experiences, told in monosyllabic prose, works that were like skeletons of Hemingway's books, without the care and finish which at his best invested his writing with elemental dignity. A reaction set in against the whole school of writing that he had launched. When his novel about the second World War, *Across the River and into the Trees,* appeared in 1950, it was greeted with an adversely critical press almost without parallel in American literature. While articles on the end of his career as a novelist were still appearing, however, he published *The Old Man and the Sea,* an almost perfect story of an aging Cuban fisherman which took its place among the masterpieces of short American fiction.

Modern American fiction has been largely realistic. There were exceptions like Francis Scott Fitzgerald (1896–1950), famous for his romantic novels of the jazz age, especially *This Side of Paradise* (1920), and Thomas Wolfe (1900–1938), whose long, intensely subjective family story, *Look Homeward, Angel!,* was published in 1929. Sherwood Anderson (1876–1941) was a businessman who gave up his paint factory in Ohio to become a writer and began his career in middle age. Famous for his tales of small-town life in *Winesburg, Ohio* (1919), Anderson cast a curious, vague half-light over familiar American scenes that left them like a haunting and shadowy reflection of reality. But these writers were exceptions; by and large, from the end of the Civil War to the second World War, the dominant note in American fiction was realistic, and writers strove for a photographic representation of the life around them.

And in that representation there was a gradual lessening of the hope and confidence that had sustained American writers in the early days of American literature. The doubt and distrust that Emerson noted grew stronger and deepened to despair. By and large, American realistic novelists painted a panorama of human distress, of wasted and broken lives, purposeless suffering and preventable misery against a background of crowded and dreary cities or drab and lonely farms. Faith in progress, belief that American democracy would lead the way to a peaceful world, confidence in the eternal value of an attempt to build a new society based on human equality—all these vanished from American imaginative writing at the very time the United States, in material terms, became one of the powerful nations of the world. There have been few bodies of writing in the whole history of literature as bleak and forbidding, as hopeless and grim and despairing, as the realistic fiction of the United States in this period.

A single major work attempted to reverse the imaginative current. Strangely enough, it was a work based upon American literature itself. In 1932, Van Wyck Brooks began a cycle of books analyzing the writing of the American past with a view of its meaning to the present. At first glance, the effort seemed quixotic. What could there be, in a study of Longfellow and Emerson, of Hawthorne and Thoreau and Emily Dickinson, that would have significance in a world faced with war and depression, or with new kinds of scientific warfare that threatened the end of mankind? Yet as the five volumes of Van Wyck Brooks' history appeared, it became evident that the messages of the great American writers had not lost their meaning, and that to restate them in modern terms reaffirmed the old values of democracy as powerfully as they had been expressed before.

Van Wyck Brooks was born in Plainfield, New Jersey, in 1886, was graduated from Harvard, became a newspaperman in London, an editor in New York, and was the most distinguished literary critic in America when he began his history. His reputation rested on acute studies of the American cultural inheritance: *The Wine of the Puritans* (1909), *America's Coming-of-Age* (1915), *The Ordeal of Mark Twain* (1920). When he finished his biography of Emerson in 1932, he set about making a unified critical appraisal of the whole of American literature, beginning with *The Flowering of New England* (1936), which opened the study at a moment when the native American genius seemed to have reached its highest point of development.

The history of this book is as extraordinary as any in American critical writing. Virtually a survey of New England intellectual life, informal in its tone yet profoundly serious in its appraisal of the thought of the New England writers, it became a popular favorite, remaining a best seller for more than a year. There was nothing sensational in it, except in the sense that the rediscovery of the meaning of these writers was in itself sensational. When the last of the five-volume work, *The Confident Years*, appeared in 1954, the sales of all of the books amounted to a million copies.

Brooks' great cycle of books is one of the major achievements of the American imagination. It is comparable to the work of William Prescott and Francis Parkman in boldness, originality and scholarship, and superior to their work in artistry. In *The World of Washington Irving*, Brooks reviewed the forgotten beginnings of our national literature, carrying the story up through the death of Poe. *The Flowering of New England*, though published first, came second in the chronological sequence of the history, an inclusive, authoritative, inspiring book which contained, especially in the chapters on Emerson in Concord and Hawthorne in Salem, passages that equaled the work of Emerson and Hawthorne. The third volume, *New England: Indian Summer* (1940), dealt with the time when the first generation of New England men of letters, the great figures of Longfellow, Prescott and their contemporaries, had passed on and a new generation that had absorbed their influence faced the new social order that was growing with industrialism. *The Times of Melville and Whitman* opened with the literary scene in New York while Washington Irving was still alive and closed with a chapter on Mark Twain in his Hartford home. The final volume, *The Confident Years*, spanned the period between Hamlin Garland's first book and the novels of Faulkner and Hemingway.

Brooks' studies opened a new period in American critical writing, and perhaps a new period in American literature. They revealed that native American literature is a wellspring of inspiration, and they redefined the American tradition in terms that had a concrete application for the present. American writers lived again in these books, and their wisest words echoed unforgettably, summoning up again the promise of America that Herman Melville put into words: "We are the heirs of all time, and with all nations we divide our inheritance. On this Western Hemisphere all tribes and peoples are forming into one federated whole; and there is a future which shall see the estranged children of Adam restored as to the old hearthstone in Eden."

Index

Across the River and into the Trees, 184

Adventures of Captain Bonneville, 30

Adventures of Tom Sawyer, 122, 126, 128-130

Alhambra, The, 38, 163

Alias Jimmy Valentine, 152

Alice Doane's Appeal, 45

America's Coming of Age, 186

Amory, Susan (Mrs. William Prescott), 40

Anderson, Sherwood, 184

As I Lay Dying, 182

Astoria, 30

Babbitt, 179

Battles and Leaders of the Civil War, 139

Before Adam, 170

Benito Cereno, 97

Big Two-Hearted River, 183

Billy Budd, 98

Black Cat, The, 68

Blithedale Romance, The, 54, 56

Book of Roses, The, 110

Bracebridge Hall, 28

Bridge, Horatio, 52, 53

Brook Farm, 54, 56, 77

Brooks, Van Wyck, 14, 131, 185-187

Burning Daylight, 170

Cabbages and Kings, 157

Caldwell, Erskine, 180, 181

Call of the Wild, The, 161, 165, 170

Clarel, 98

Clemens, Olivia, 123-124, 130

Clemens, Orion, 117, 118

Clemens, Samuel (see Mark Twain)

Clemm, Mrs. Maria, 66

Clemm, Virginia (Mrs. Edgar Allan Poe), 68

Colonel Sellers, 124

Conduct of Life, The, 78

Confident Years, The, 186

Connecticut Yankee in King Arthur's Court, A, 126, 128, 173

Conquest of Granada, 29

Conquest of Mexico, 45

Conquest of Peru, 45

Conspiracy of Pontiac, The, 108

Cooper, James Fenimore, 9-21, 96, 116, 173, 175, 176

Cooper, Judge, 11, 13

Count Frontenac and New France, 110

Crane, Stephen, 135-145

Deerslayer, The, 14, 19

De Lancy, Susan (Mrs. James Fenimore Cooper), 12

De Gayangos, Pascual, 44

Descent into the Maelstrom, A, 67, 70

Dial, The, 81, 86

Dickinson, Emily, 185
Double-Dyed Deceiver, The, 155
Dos Passos, John, 179, 180
Dreiser, Theodore, 179-181

Emerson, Ralph Waldo, 75-78, 85-87, 177, 185, 186
English Traits, 78
Essays, 78
Ethan Brand, 56

Fable, A, 182
Fall of the House of Usher, The, 65
Fanshawe, 52
Farewell to Arms, 183
Farrell, James, 180, 181
Faulkner, William, 181, 182, 187
Ferdinand and Isabella, 43
Financier, The, 179
Fitzgerald, Francis Scott, 184
Flowering of New England, The, 186, 187
For Whom the Bell Tolls, 184
France and England in the New World, 109

Garland, Hamlin, 178, 187
Gift of the Magi, The, 154
Gilded Age, The, 124
God's Little Acre, 181
Gold Bug, The, 61, 62, 65
Graham's Magazine, 68
Grant, General Ulysses S., 94, 125
Gray Champion, The, 55
Great Stone Face, The, 55
Green, Tobias, 93, 94
Griswold, Rufus, 69

Half-Century of Conflict, A, 111
Harte, Bret, 119

Hawthorne, Betsy Manning (Hawthorne's mother), 49
Hawthorne, Elizabeth (Hawthorne's sister), 53
Hawthorne, Nathaniel, 50-57, 87, 94, 97, 98, 176, 182, 185
Hazard of New Fortunes, A, 178
Heart of the West, 157
Hemingway, Ernest, 181, 183, 184, 187
Henry, O., (see O. Henry)
History of the Conquest of Mexico, 45
History of the Conquest of Peru, 45
History of the Life and Voyages of Christopher Columbus, 29
History of the Navy of the United States, 17, 18
History of Philip the Second, 46
History of the Reign of Ferdinand and Isabella, 41-43
Holding Up a Train, 155
Hollow of the Three Hills, The, 55
Holmes, Oliver Wendell, 56
Home as Found, 15
Horseshoe Robinson, 67
House of the Seven Gables, The, 54
Howells, William Dean, 178, 179
Huckleberry Finn, 122, 125-128

Innocents Abroad, The, 120
Irving, Peter, 26
Irving, Sarah Sanders, 25
Irving, Washington, 23-33, 45, 46, 163, 187
Irving, William, 26
Israel Potter, 97

James, Henry, 143
Jennie Gerhardt, 179
Jesuits in North America, The, 110
John Barleycorn, 170

Kennedy, John, 67

Langdon, Charles, 120
Langdon, Olivia (Mrs. Samuel Clemens), 120, 121, 130
La Salle and the Discovery of the Great West, 110
Last of the Mohicans, The, 11, 13, 21
Legend of Sleepy Hollow, The, 28
Letters of Jonathan Oldstyle, Gent., 26
Lewis, Sinclair, 179
Life of Oliver Goldsmith, 31
Life on the Mississippi, 122, 124, 126
Light in August, 182
Lionel Lincoln, 10
Little Norske, A, 178
Lives of Mahomet and His Successors, 31
London, Charmian, 167, 168
London, Jack, 161-170, 177
London, John, 163
Longfellow, Henry Wadsworth, 51, 94, 185, 187

Maggie, A Girl of the Streets, 138, 142
Main Street, 179
Main Traveled Roads, 178
Marble Faun, The, 54
Mardi, 94
Marquis and Miss Sally, The, 155

Martin Eden, 169
Melville, Herman, 91-99, 111, 163, 176, 181, 187
Melville, Malcolm, 99
Melville, Major Thomas, 92
Miracle of Lava Canyon, The, 152
Moby Dick, 92, 95-98
Montcalm and Wolfe, 111
Mosquitoes, 181
Mosses from an Old Manse, 54
Murders in the Rue Morgue, The, 68
Mystery of Marie Roget, The, 68

Nature, 76
New England: Indian Summer, 187
Notions of the Americans, 15

Oak Openings, 19
O. Henry, 149-158
Old Man and the Sea, The, 184
Old Regime in Canada, The, 110
Omoo, 94
Open Boat, The, 140
Options, 157
Ordeal of Mark Twain, The, 186
Oregon Trail, The, 105, 106, 108, 109
Our Old Home, 54

Parkman, Francis, 103-112, 177, 186
Pathfinder, The, 13, 19
Peabody, Sophia (Mrs. Nathaniel Hawthorne), 54
Personal Recollections of Joan of Arc, 128
Philip the Second, 46
Pierre, 97
Pilot, The, 14, 173

Pioneers of France in the New World, 109
Pit and the Pendulum, The, 68
Piazza Tales, 97
Poe, David, 62, 64
Poe, Edgar Allan, 61-71
Poe, Rosalie, 62, 67
Poe, William Henry Leonard, 62-67
Porter, Margaret (daughter of O. Henry), 149, 156
Porter, William Sidney (see O. Henry)
Precaution, 13
Prescott, William Hickling, 31, 37-46, 110, 186, 187
Prince and the Pauper, The, 128
Pudd'nhead Wilson, 130
Pylon, 182

Ransom of Red Chief, The, 155
Red Badge of Courage, The, 135, 136, 139, 141, 143, 145
Redburne, 93, 94
Representative Men, 78
Retrieved Reformation, A, 152
Rip Van Winkle, 28
Rise of Silas Lapham, 178
Road of Destiny, 157
Roughing It, 124, 126

Salmagundi Papers, The, 27
Sanctuary, 182
Sartoris, 181, 182
Scarlet Letter, The, 54, 55
Sea Lions, The, 19
Sea Wolf, The, 165, 166
Seven Tales of My Native Land, 53
Shaw, Elizabeth (Mrs. Herman Melville), 94

Shaw, Quincy, 105, 108
Sister Carrie, 179
Sketch Book, The, 28, 30
Snow Image, The, 54
Society and Solitude, 78
Soldiers Pay, 181
Springtime a la Carte, 153
Star Rover, The, 170
Strictly Business, 157
Studs Lonigan, 181
Sun Also Rises, The, 183
Swallow Barn, 67

Tamerlane and Other Poems, 65
Tanglewood Tales, 54
Tell-Tale Heart, The, 68
This Side of Paradise, 184
Thoreau, Henry David, 77, 78-85, 185
Thoreau, John, 80
Three Soldiers, 180
Times of Melville and Whitman, The, 187
Titan, The, 179
To Have and to Have Not, 184
Tobacco Road, 181
Tom Sawyer, 122, 126, 128-130
Tour of the Prairies, 30
Tramp Abroad, A, 126
Trimmed Lamp, The, 159
Twain, Mark, 21, 115-131, 173, 176, 182, 187
Twice-Told Tales, 53
Typee, 94

U.S.A., 179, 180

Valley of the Moon, The, 170
Vassal Morton, 108
Vision of the Fountain, The, 50
Voice of the City, The, 157

INDEX

Voyages and Discoveries of the Companions of Columbus, 30

Walden, 79
Week on the Concord and Merrimack Rivers, A, 81
Whirligigs, 157
White Fang, 170
White-Jacket, 95

William Wilson, 69
Wine of the Puritans, 186
Winesburg, Ohio, 184
Wolfe, Thomas, 184
Wonder Book, The, 54
World of Washington Irving, The, 186

Young Goodman Brown, 55